Your 'go to' source for STUPID FAST® motorcycle parts

BST Carbon Fiber Wheels

- 40-60% weight savings vs. OEM
- Unparalleled aesthetic upgrade
- DOT E approved for street use
- Reduces road noise and vibration
- Reduces rider / passenger fatigue
- **Multiple Finish Options:** Gloss, Satin, Matte, and Colored Ink

  (Blue, Red, Green, Orange, Gold, or Black)

Performance FXR Swingarm

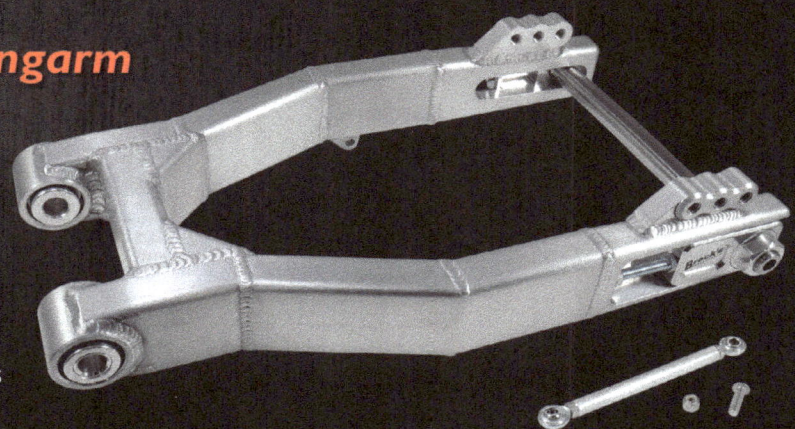

- Handcrafted 6061-T6 aluminum 0-3" extended swingarm
- Proudly designed, machined, and assembled in the USA
- Spherical bearings preinstalled
- Features 3-position shock mounts

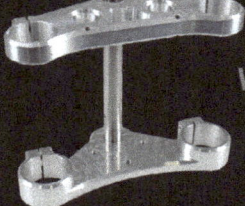

Visit BrocksPerformance.com for a complete listing of FXR products.
Triple Tree Clamps, Fork Extensions, Air Cleaners, Shocks, and More!

BrocksPerformance.com
(937) 912-0054

Harley-Davidson FXR Bible

by Timothy Remus

Published by:
Wolfgang Publications, Inc.
P.O. Box 223
Stillwater, MN 55082

ISBN: 978-1-941064-55-9
Printed in USA

Legals

First published in 2020 by Wolfgang Publications Inc.
P.O. Box 223
Stillwater, MN 55082

© Timothy Remus 2020

All rights reserved. With the exception of quoting brief passages for the purposes of review no part of this publication may be reproduced without prior written permission from the publisher.

The information in this book is true and complete to the best of our knowledge. All recommendations are made without any guarantee on the part of the author or publisher, who also disclaim any liability incurred in connection with the use of this data or specific details.

We recognize that some words, model names and designations, for example, mentioned herein, are the property of the trademark holder. We them for identification purposes only. This is not an official publication.

ISBN: 978-1-941064-55-9

Table of Contents

Acknowledgments 5
Introduction 6
Chapter One FXR History *by Chaz* 7
Chapter Two The FXR Frame *Q&A with Skeeter Todd* 15
Chapter Three Electrical *Q&A with Jeff Zielinski owner and founder of NAMZ* . . 17
Chapter Four Drivetrain Choices for your FXR *Q&A with Mark Shadley* 23
Chapter Five The Importance of a Clean Title *Q&A with Rob Kenney* 27
Chapter Six The FXR Shows *Joe Mielke* 31
Chapter Seven Planning *The Forgotten Step* 36
Chapter Eight How It All Started *by Bill Radcliffe* 41
Chapter Nine A New/Old Luxury Liner *Arlen's Dream* 43
Chapter Ten A Donnie Smith FXR 48
Chapter Eleven Neil's Hot Rod FXR 53
Chapter Twelve Not Another Custom 58
Chapter Thirteen FXR2 by Ness 63
Chapter Fourteen Timeless Styling 67
Chapter Fifteen All about the Motor 72
Chapter Sixteen Lean and Mean 77
Chapter Seventeen Road Runner 82
Chapter Eighteen Arlen & Arlin 88
Chapter Nineteen Did it Myself 91
Chapter Twenty Top Shelf 96
Chapter Twenty One Aged Like a Fine Wine 101
Chapter Twenty Two First Time Custom 106
Chapter Twenty Three An 'RT with Attitude 113
Chapter Twenty Four Dream Machine 119
Chapter Twenty Five FXR CVO Specials 125
Chapter Twenty Six A Replacement for the FXR 127
Chapter Twenty Seven Sport Touring Dyna 129
Chapter Twenty Eight One Woman's Hot Rod 133
Chapter Twenty Nine A Pro Builds One For Himself 136
Chapter Thirty A Performance Dyna 140

Acknowledgments

I have the benefit of multiple friends in the V-Twin aftermarket and I definitely did tap into that reserve of knowledge in assembling this book. The list is long, so I chose to simply mention each one with their contribution. There likely are a few I missed, you know who are. And, as they say, errors are mine, not theirs. Seriously, this book would not exist without all these contributors – many thanks to one and all.

~ Timothy Remus

Arlin Fatland – Information
Brian Gall – Pics
Hank Ham – Chapter 05A
Chaz - History & more
Mike Johnson – Chapters 25 & 26
Nigel Kennedy – Pics
Rob Kenney – Chapter 05
J. R. Lopes – Pics
Doug Mitchel – Pics
Joe Mielke – Chapter 06

Kurt Peterson – Pics, copy, & moral support
Bill Radcliffe – Copy
Mike Savage – Pics & moral support
Mark Shadley – Chapter 04
Neil Ryan - Year by Year 01A
Skeeter Todd – Chapter 02
Jim Waggaman – Pics
Jeff Zielinski – Chapter 03
All Owners & Builders – Copy, pics, & moral support

Source Guide

Baker Drivetrain
Gearsets, including 6-speed kits for factory FXR cases.
https://bakerdrivetrain.com/

Biker's Choice
Giant catalog.
www.bikerschoice.com

Blackmore Manufacturing
Frame-mounted mid-size fairings.
https://wedgefairing.com
info@wedgefaring.com

Brock's Performance
A long list of performance components including Carbon wheels, triple trees, swingarms and more…
https://brocksperformance.com

Deadbeat Customs
Abundant aftermarket parts for FXRs & Dynas, from bars and risers to 2-into-1 exhaust.
DeadbeatCustoms.com

Deviant Fabrications
Oil pan for Twin Cam/FXR conversion.
https://www.deviantfabrications.com/

Drag Specialties
Huge Huge Catalog.
https://www.dragspecialties.com

Donnie Smith Custom Cycles
Fabrication & bike building.
Donnie Smith Custom Cycles - Facebook

Dave Perewitz
Fabrication & bike building.
Perewitz - Facebook

Klock Werks
Parts, service, fabrication.
https://www.getklocked.com/399-2/

JD Customs & Fab
FXR fairing, clam-shell bags etc.
jdcustomsandfab@gmail.com

Lil' Evil
Bike building including painting and engine building.
Lil' Evil Inkorpor8ted - Facebook

Shadley Bros.
Fabrication, bike building & service.
https://www.shadleybros.com

Shooters Images Inc. - Don Kates
Photographer for Rick Ward's Dyna, specialized in motorcycles.
don@shootersimages.com
don@dakates.com

The Fxr Garage
The Fxr Garage Public Group | Facebook
Ward Performance
Rick Ward is well known as the man to see for porting - also engine building and upgrades.
http://www.wardperformance.com/

West End Motorsports
Stabilizers for Dyna suspensions.
www.westendmotorsports.com

Introduction

What it is

This book is essentially an in-depth look at the motorcycle many people feel is the best machine ever built by Harley-Davidson – the FXR - and its cousin the Dyna.

The FXR Bible starts with History, told partly as a narrative and partly as a chart that calls out the major changes and improvements to the FXR – Year by Year. And if there is one thing, one part that defines the FXR, it would have to be the Frame - with its rubber mounts and that signature triangular section under the seat. Thus the book includes an essay explaining why that particular frame works as well as it does.

And because you can't ride a bike (at least for very long) without a license plate, it's necessary to talk about the Paperwork needed to get that license plate, especially important with scratch-built bikes.

Next comes a section on Electricity – or rather, the components and harnesses that move the electrons around the motorcycle so it will start and run and have lights at night.

Fans of the FXR and participants in the renaissance of interest in the FXR owe a big debt to Joe Mielke – so I gave him a chapter of his own - Joe is the rider and enthusiast who brought us the FXR Shows.

Before leaving what I call the Front Section of the book I've put together a chapter called simply - Planning – meant as an aid to riders with a dream of building a kick-ass FXR of their own. There are times when it pays to slow down and think first.

The balance of the book is features of a large group of custom FXRs, and a smaller group of Dynas. The idea is to learn from examples. The features focus on the initial dream and how that was achieved. Some are 'RTs ready to take on the highway, and others are back-to-basics hot rods meant for ripping around town and down the quarter-mile.

My hope is that the FXR Bible achieves my three goals:

Entertain - with photos and stories about our favorite topic: custom motorcycles.

Educate – by sharing the knowledge and wisdom of some very intelligent and motivated builders.

Motivate – anyone with half a notion to personalize the bike they ride, or build one from the ground up.

All because there is almost nothing better than rolling down your favorite road on a motorcycle that's truly your own.

Chapter One

FXR History

by Chaz

In the late 1970's and early 1980's Harley Davidson found their motorcycles lagging in the market. Years of minimal investment and innovation had left Harley behind the market in sales and production. In order to fill the demands from the base customers, Harley engineers felt the need to replace the aging FLH (Electra Glide) frame which had been in production since 1958. The result was the introduction of the new FLT (Tour Glide) frame in 1980. The new frame was longer, had triangulated re-enforcement under the seat and provided for rubber mounting of the motor and transmission. The end result was a smoother, more comfortable and better handling touring bike.

In 1980 Harley Davidsons cruiser bikes, the FXE (Super Glide) and FXS (Low Rider) were still being built on the old FLH frame. By 1982 Harley Davidson introduced a new frame to fill in the space between the Sportster and the big twin touring bikes. The Result was the FXR. The FXR frame was shorter and lighter than the outdated FLH/FX frame. It featured the triangulated re-enforcement design and a square backbone like its big brother the FLT. It also incorporated rubber motor

Like all the FXRs manufactured from 1984 to the end of the line, this 1984 FXRT is powered by an Evo, with the early version of the five-speed transmission, and the belt final drive.

Doug Mitchel

mounting and was designed for Harley's existing big twin motors and the new FLT transmission and primary. The FXR frame was not just a downsized FLT frame.

The new frame was designed by a team of Harley engineers which included Bob Leroy and Erik Buell. The frame featured the same elastomer, thee-point mounting in the motor cradle and triangulated mid-frame structure as the new FLT. These features allowed the Shovelhead motor and 5-speed transmission from the FLT to be used in the new FXR without any modification. That's where the similarities end. The frame utilized stamped steel instead of cast components for bracing and assembly, in order to lower both cost and weight. The geometries of the frame made for faster handling and increased high-speed stability. Assembly for the frames was labor intensive. Robotic welding was not in use at the time so all FXR frames were hand welded. When the new frame was introduced many riders were skeptical. Despite the skeptics, however, the FXR quickly became known as the best handling bike Harley Davidson ever made. In fact, the FXR still enjoys that reputation to this day.

The FXR filled the gap between the big Harley-Davidson touring bikes and the entry-level Sportster. The FXR offered big twin comfort and performance in smaller, lighter, smoother, fast handling machine.

The FLT, though seen as an ugly duck today, was the bike and frame that paved the way for the rubber-mounts to follow – including the FXR, and the Baggers that became the bike-of-choice for so many riders.

1st Generation

1982-1984. [Editor's note: Some features were in flux on early FXRs, the following paragraph is essentially my own.]

The first generation FXR's used a combination of existing FLT and Sportster parts. The basic configuration was the 80 inch Shovelhead motor with the FLT early five-speed transmission. 1982 FXRs came with the Shovel, early five-speed and enclosed chain drive to the rear wheel. The 1983s came with the Shovel and early five-speed, but the final drive style was dependent on the model - FXRTs used the enclosed chain, while the rest of the '83 FXRs used the then-new belt final drive. 1984 FXRs used the new Evo motor and early five-speed, but followed the final drive pattern seen in the 1983 models – it depended on the model. All of these early FXRs utilized the 35mm Sportster front forks and 10 inch disc brakes front and rear.

The original chain drive on the FXRs was an enclosed oil-bath chain from the FLT. While being a maintenance nightmare, the chains lasted forever. The FLT transmission had its own problems. It used the same keyed, tapered shaft and small bearing case as the FLT's. The primary used the dry clutch which made primary maintenance tricky and required special tools. The 10 inch brakes were weak on stopping power and prone to caliper leakage and brake fade with hard use. The first generation FXR's used the 35mm Showa Sportster front forks. These front forks were generally considered too weak and flexible for a big twin motorcycle.

Problems; chain, trans, dry clutch, brakes.

Models; Super Glide II, Low Glide, FXRT.

2nd Generation

1985-1986. The 2nd generation FXR's saw several improvements. The new 80 inch Evo motor, belt drive and upgraded 11.5 inch brakes provided very desirable reliability and performance enhancements for the rider. The primary and transmission also received an upgrade. The 2nd generation FXR Transmission cases have larger bearings and the case is specific to the FXR. The dry clutch was gone and the standard wet clutch from the touring models was the new standard. The FX series bikes were gone in 1985 and Harley-Davidson used the original names of Super Glide and Low Rider. Harley-Davidson also kept the FXRT in the lineup as well as introducing the FXRP. The FXRP was a mid-weight police cruiser designed to compete against the Kawasaki Z1-P in both cost and performance.

There were some on going issues with the FXRs. The transmission retained the tapered, keyed main shaft even though the main shaft bearing and transmission case had been improved. The 2nd generation transmission case and primary were specific to the 1985-86 FXRs, which made replacement costly. The FXRs still used the lightweight 35mm Front forks which flexed under stress.

Problems: trans, clutch.

Models: Super Glide, Low Rider, FXRT, FXRD, FXRP.

3rd Generation

1987-1994. The 3rd generation FXR's brought many improvements and cemented the FXR's reputation as Harley's best performing and handling Harley-Davidson. The front forks were upgraded to the new 39mm Showa forks. The rear shocks were repositioned to improve

The first FXRs, 1982 and '83, came with the Shovelhead – and have become classics. Riders are scrounging for all those stock parts that we threw away in the 80s in order to bring 'em back to stock.

With input from Eric Buell, the "ugly" FXRT was designed with help from time spent in a wind tunnel. Bags too were unique, with their clam-shell design and overall shape.
Doug Mitchel

1984 was the first year for the Evo, and where better to make use of Harley's new motor than in the "touring" version of the bike introduced in 1982. Doug Mitchel

traction and rebound. The transmission was upgraded with a splined main shaft and now used the touring case. The primary was also switched to the touring model.

Models: Super Glide, Low Rider, Low Rider Convertible, Low Rider Custom, FXRT, FXRP.

Note: All CVO Special FXR's (FXR2, FXR3, FXR4) are 3rd Generation.

The Models

FXR, 1982-1994. The Base model FXR was equipped with an 80 Cubic Inch motor, Evo introduced in mid-1984. Enclosed chain until mid-1984. Cast wheels (19" front, 16" rear), single disc brake front and rear, pillow seat.

Super Glide II, FXRS 1983-84. All had the Shovelhead motor and enclosed chain. Laced wheels (19" front, 16" rear), dual disc front, single disc rear, pillow seat.

Low Glide, FXLR 1983-86. Shovelhead motor and enclosed chain until mid-1984. Cast wheels (19" front, 16" rear), single disc front and rear, pillow seat.

Super Glide, FXRS 1985-93. The Super glide became Harley Davidsons's mid-size performance motorcycle. All were produced with the Evo V2 motor and 5-speed transmissions. Available with either laced or cast wheels (19' front, 16" rear), with dual disc front brakes and single disc rear brake, pillow seats, belt drive.

Low Rider Custom, FXLR 1987-1993. 21 inch laced front wheel, 16 inch disc rear wheel. Evo V2 motor, 5-speed transmission, belt drive,

Harley-Davidson wasted no time in outfitting their new mid-size bike with equipment appealing to the Police and Highway Patrol - especially when the FXR came stock with the Evo. Though most of the Police bikes came with the FXRP fairing, this example carries only the windshield. Doug Mitchel

forward controls, smooth tank, offset filler, gauges mounted in tank console, pillow seat with passenger back rest, single disc brakes front and rear.

Low Rider and Low Rider Convertible, FXLR 1987-1994. Evo V2 motor, 5-speed transmission, single front and rear disc brakes, riser mounted gauges, cast wheels (19" front, 16" rear), belt drive, mid controls. Convertible models included easily detachable leather saddlebags and a detachable windshield.

Sport Glide, FXRT 1983-1992. This was the first FXR variant. The bikes had the shovelhead motor and enclosed chain until mid-1984. The FXRT was the first civilian model to have the Evo V2 and belt drive in mid-1984. The FXRP received Evo in late 1983. The FXRT was essentially a Super Glide with a fairing and saddlebags. It had cast wheels (19" front, 16" rear), dual disc front and single disc rear brakes, riser mounted gauges and pillow seat. It also included the Nova project fairing and clamshell saddlebags, a rear luggage rack, passenger back rest and tour pack.

Sport Glide Deluxe, FXRD 1986 only. Despite popular opinion, this was a one-year bike. The FXRD had all the features of the FXRT except as noted. The FXRD had the gauges moved to the fairing along with a factory stereo and glove boxes. The motorcycle also included fairing lowers. The FXRD was available in both standard and Grand Touring trim packages.

J.R.'s 1987 FXR is essentially stock, including the laced front wheel and cast rear, sheet metal and paint.

By 1987 belt drive to the rear wheel was taken for granted. Evo motor is stock, at least externally.

Police Model, FXRP 1983-1994. The FXRP was introduced and rushed to market to get Harley Davidson back into the police market. The FXRP was a mid-weight police cruiser designed to compete against the Kawasaki Z1-P in both cost and performance. The FXRP was originally produced with a windshield and specially designed hard bags. In mid-1984 the FXRP was offered with a modified FXRT (Nova) fairing. All FXRPs had the Evo V2 motor, 5-speed transmission, belt final drive, cast wheels (19" front, 16" rear) with single disc brakes front and rear. The standard configuration was birch white paint, red and blues in the front, red pole light in the rear and radio box. As with other Harley Davidson Police models, the FXRP could be ordered with department specific custom paint. Other unique FXRP parts include the oversize dash to house radio controls, the siren mounted on the engine guard and the spring mounted seat. As the FXRP's aged in the police ranks they were sold on the civilian market. These bikes became the basis for many of the FXR custom motorcycles that are still around today.

Special Editions. The FXR CVO releases were the first of the Harley Davidson CVO models. It is very appropriate that the first CVO head was Bob Leroy who headed the original FXR design team. After the end of standard production of the FXR, there was a steady demand from enthusiasts to re-introduce the motorcycle. Harley Davidson decided to produce a limited release through the newly formed CVO division.

All CVO FXR's were built on new frames manufactured in 1999. The popular rumor is the frames were left over from previous production runs. The CVO FXR's were updated with a wiring harness that had the latest connectors as well as the current model brakes and controls. The CVO editions were also equipped with most of the chrome and accessories available for the FXR in the Harley Accessories Catalog.

Customizing the FXR

The FXR is a popular motorcycle to customize. Modifications range from bolting on a chrome accessory or changing the seat; to the installation of a S&S 145 cubic inch, nitrous fed monster built by Crazy John Markwald. Or the turbo charged FXRs built by Nick Trask. There are "Clubber Style" FXRs with tall risers or T-bars, short exhausts and performance suspensions. There are also FXRs which have been lowered and setup like the "California Diggers". There have also been FXRs setup as Adventure bikes by Randy Aron of Cycle Visions and Joe Mielke.

The most common modifications to the FXR are for performance. Motor mods such as exhaust, air cleaner and camshaft are the first place many FXR owners go. Some owners go a little farther and replace the aging EVO motors with aftermarket upgrades from S&S, TP and other manufacturers. The latest performance trend in FXRs is to install Twin Cam motors and six speed transmissions from the newer generation of touring models.

This is what a 1983 FXRT looks like – with a bit of extra chrome, too-tall risers and aftermarket seat. The bike is otherwise correct in terms of wheels, sheet metal, fairing and bags.

Common suspension modifications include high performance shock absorbers, replacing older (1982-1986) 35mm front forks with later 39mm forks or even 49mm forks from the Dyna series bikes. Brock Performance even provides parts to use inverted sport bike front forks and radial disc brakes on FXRs. Skeeter Todd built a 124 cubic inch S&S twin cam bike using inverted forks, a Brock performance lengthened and reinforced swing arm, radial brakes and carbon fiber wheels.

The list of what can be done with FXRs is endless. The limit is literally the builder's imagination and financial resources. One of the latest trends has been to build more and more FXRs in a 'resto-mod, clubber style" touring FXRs. These are performance built FXRs with motor, transmission and suspension mods that use the FXRT, FXRD or FXRP fairings and saddlebags. This has created a demand for the FXR variant fairings and saddlebags. Many original parts were simply thrown away in the mid 1990's. There is now a growing aftermarket segment which is reproducing the fairings, saddlebags and other parts from the factory touring models.

The Evolution Motor: Saving Harley Davidson

No discussion of the FXR could be complete without discussing the Evo V2 motor. In the mid 1970's Harley Davidson/AMF worked with Porsche to improve manufacturing technology and product performance. The lurking gorilla in the room was the aging Shovelhead motor. The late variants of the motor were plagued with a lack of reliability, performance and leaked worse than the previous models. Part of the problem was the aging machinery at the factory. Another issue was the use of cast iron heads and cylinders on the aluminum motor cases.

When Harley Davidson successfully bought out AMF in 1981 the road was open for improvement. With better machining, the use of aluminum heads and cylinders and some applied innovation, Harley Davison introduced the Evo V2 motor in 1984. By the end of 1984 the Evo motor was used in the entire big twin lineup. The Evo motor design was eventually used for the Sportster motor as well.

It's hard to find FXRs that are truly stock. Chris' FXR4 retains the frame and running gear, factory wheels, and sheet metal. The seat, paint and a few other items are not factory.

FXR Year by Year

Major Mechanical Changes

by Neil Ryan with input from Chaz, Skeeter and Mike Savage

1982 and 1983

The first FXRs came with the Shovel engine and a dry clutch system. Shovels used Bendix carburetor. 1982 and 1983 used the five-speed tranny – the early five-speed transmissions came with the tapered outpt shaft, which is not as strong as later versions of the five-speed. Strong clutches designed to fit on the tapered shaft are hard to find. The inner primary on these are all alone. They're hard to find and expensive if you need one.

1982 models came with the enclosed chain final drive. 1983 was the first FXR with belt final drive. Belt drive was used from 1983 to the end of production.1983, was last year for the Shovel.

1984

Evo engines for all FXRs from here to end of production. All Evos used Kehin carburetors.

1984 to 1986

No more dry primary - wet primary/clutch from this point forward. Five-speed transmissions continue, and retain the tapered output shaft. 1984 to 1985, fender struts change, part of a subtle frame change.

1987

Milwaukee changed the trap door and clutch mechanism on the transmissions. From 1987 forward the five-speed transmissions used the stronger and more modern five-speed transmission with splined output shaft. 35mm fork tubes were changed to 39mm. Rear shock position is changed.

90 to 94

From 1990 to the end of standard production in 1994 there were few serious mechanice changes.

CVO FXRs

FXR2 (Super Glide 2) Came with mid-controls and highway pegs. Spoked, 19 inch front wheel, cast, 16 inch rear wheel. Dual discs on front.

FXR3 Came with mid-controls and cast wheels, 19 and 16 inches. Contrast paint, disc brakes on both ends.

FXR4, Came in two colors; 300 in Candy Tangerine, and 600 in Screaming Yellow Pearl.

Spoked, 19 inch front wheel, 16 inch cast rear wheel. Twin discs on the front using the new (4-piston) calipers. Came with mid-controls and a set of forward pegs. [Note: See Chapter 25 for more informaion on the CVO FXRs.]

Chapter Two

The FXR Frame

Q&A with Skeeter Todd

What's so special about the FXR? The rigidity of the frame and the amount of abuse they take without dying. The FXR is one of the first Harleys that was built on function not style. Function and performance are hard to achieve.

The FXR uses rubber mounts, but they use a three-mount system, it's a stronger system than the two mount system used on the Dyna. Now the new dressers have four mounts, but you can do it with three.

FXRs don't get the high speed giggles. There is a check list that people use on the Facebook or blogs and it lists the things that might be wrong with a FXR if it DOES get the high speed giggles, which they don't do then.

Why did Harley-Davidson quit making the FXR? Assembly time and costs. The Dyna frame is internal, you bolt everything on to it. Faster assembly.

Is a FXR better than a Dyna? If you're looking to run a big-inch motor and run hard, then the FXR is a better choice. Or are you looking for a longer wheelbase for a better ride? Then the Dyna is probably a better choice. The FXR is a rider's bike.

What are the weaknesses of FXRs? The engine-transmission interface is weak on the Evo engines. Carlini (and others) make a torque arm that creates a solid connection between the engine and

The FXR's reputation for good handling and ability to handle big engines can be traced to the frame. Note the way the neck is very well supported, and the triangle of steel tubing at the rear – ready to absorb the stress of cornering and hard launches.

Skeeter likes to add that third mounting point for the housing that locates and supports the swingarm pivot – so the housing can't rock back and forth under a load.

The Dyna frame hangs the swingarm pivot off the back of the transmission, without tying the pivot into the frame, Editor's note: Stabilizers that firm-up the frame/engine/swingarm connection are available, see Sources.

transmission on the right side – which strengthens the connection between the engine and trans.

The original swingarm bearings were horrible. But of course there are conversion kits. Custom Cycle Engineering (and others) has kits that allow you to convert the swingarm bearings from the factory cleve blocs to spherical bearings.

What about drivetrain upgrades? You can certainly install a Twin Cam in an FXR frame. Great, cheap horsepower. There are lots of take-out 103 Dyna engine and drivetrains around for cheap money.

Tell us more about the modification you like to make to the pivot point for the swingarm. Yes, I add a third point. Anything that keeps a mount (that is supposed to be mounted solid to the frame) from flexing is a good thing. So I like to add a third mounting point to the housing for the cleve block/spherical bearing.

Final comments? There's a lot of FXR information on Facebook, like FXR's of California.

The big difference between the FXR and Dyna frames is the way the FXR ties the swingarm pivot to both the transmission and the frame.

Chapter Three

Electrical

Q&A, with Jeff Zielinski owner and founder of NAMZ.

Jeff: First give us a little background on you. Most mechanics and riders shy away from electrical work, how did you end up designing and selling electrical components and complete harness assemblies? Electrical work is in my blood. I'm the youngest of three boys; we were all into electricity and components since our father was himself an electrician. Both of my older brothers were in the electrical field, wiring houses or buildings for many years before going into management. Me, I was more into electronic devices, so in middle school I was the neighborhood guy repairing Walkmans, installing car phones and high-end car audio. But this was in addition to rebuilding dirt bikes, old cars and bicycles. Regardless, I enjoyed installing, repairing and problem solving so much that I quickly made it a career shortly after graduating from high school.

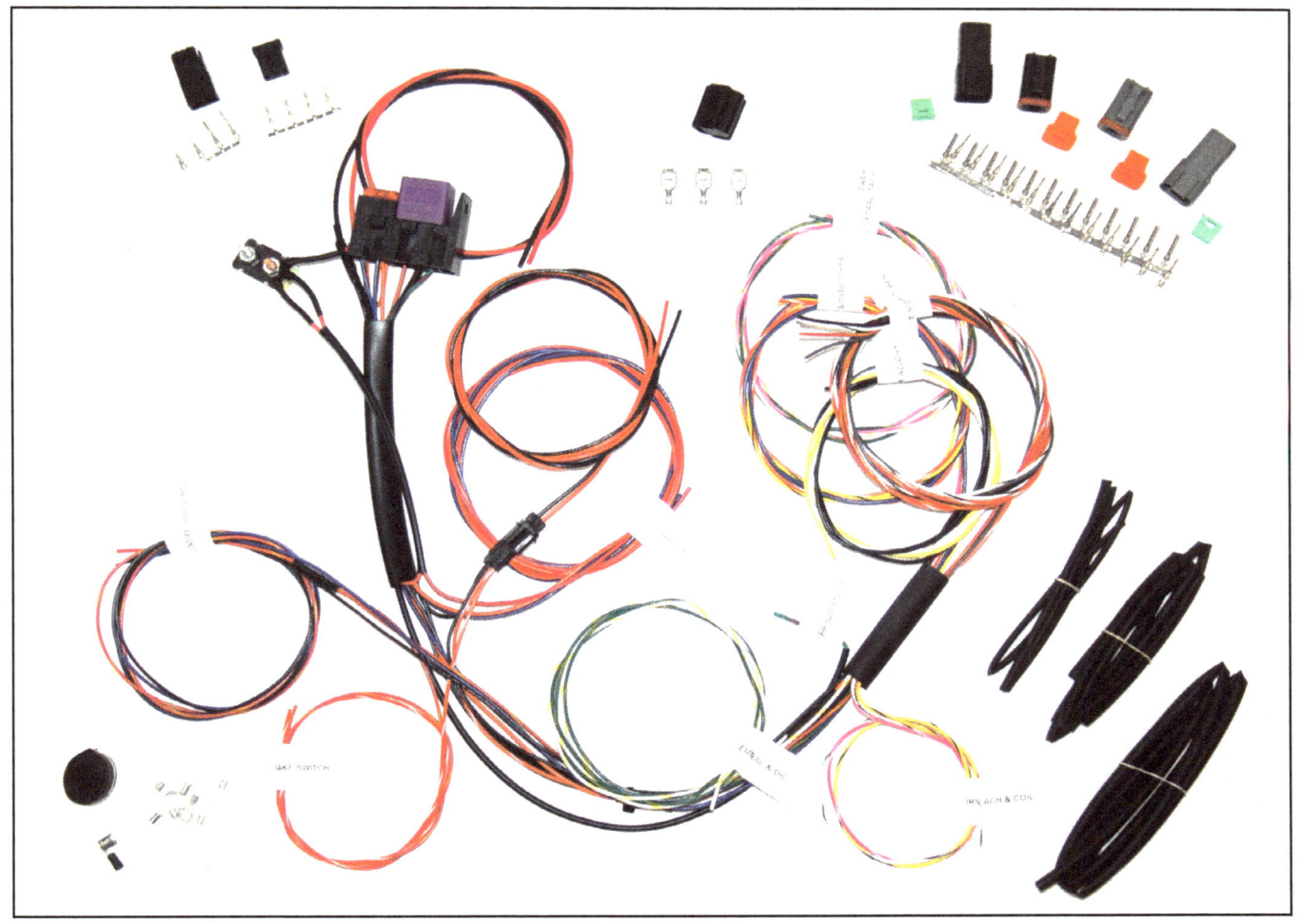

NAMZ sells a variety of harness kits, some are bare bones and some have all the bells and whistles. Shown is a Complete Bike Harness with starter relay and 3 circuits – includes shrink-wrap and heavy wires for ground and battery.

This switch assembly is mounted on a hi-mileage FXRT – been run hard and put up wet. And the original switches are still operable.

These 1996-and-up switches were spotted at a local shop. Asking price $150. Note the Deutsch connectors – which can be swapped out for earlier connector blocks and plugged in to stock FXR harnesses. NAMZ

The wireless phone industry became my career path and was the foundation for the very first harnesses I designed. I had access to wire and electronic knowledge that didn't yet exist in the motorcycle world. So my goal was to make stainless steel braided and clear coated wiring harnesses that were easy to install for the average enthusiast. That's where it all began 20+ years ago.

And how about a little information on NAMZ. When and why did you start NAMZ, what have you been able to do in terms of innovative components and parts that help riders keep their bikes on the road, that other companies couldn't or simply didn't offer?

NAMZ Started in 1998 and I made it official in 1999 by incorporating as an LLC. Just to make everyone aware, NAMZ is my nickname backwards, ZMAN. Moving on, I have eight part numbers of stainless steel braided and clear-coated harness kits and began pushing them in the Tri-State area, even up into New York on my days off. Met some great people along the way and they helped me make a modest start, but a good start nonetheless. Since my 1997 Softail was super tricked out with Arlen Ness parts and had my wiring all done up, I sent an email to Arlen Ness hoping to get their attention. No long after that email was sent, I talked with Cory Ness and our parts ended up in their

2000 parts catalog.

Along with our first part numbers, we began selling every electrical connector Harley has used since 1971. This was huge since it had never been done before. Soon every distributor in the world had NAMZ connectors to offer their customers. In 2012, NAMZ purchased Badlands Motorcycle Products out of Sparks, Nevada and implemented re-engineering of all their original designs including dozens of new modules.

In late 2018, we created Letric Lighting Co., specializing in LED lighting. Now, twenty years later, NAMZ has become a manufacturing and engineering company that specializes in motorcycle electrics – with distribution of our components around the world.

We're the only one of our kind who manufactures much of what we sell right here in the Philadelphia suburbs. Our close to 30-employees manufacture complete custom wiring harnesses, obsolete OEM harnesses, LED lighting and motorcycle electronics under our brands and for most of the US aftermarket motorcycle industry. Chances are if you buy something with a wiring harness in this industry, it came from us.

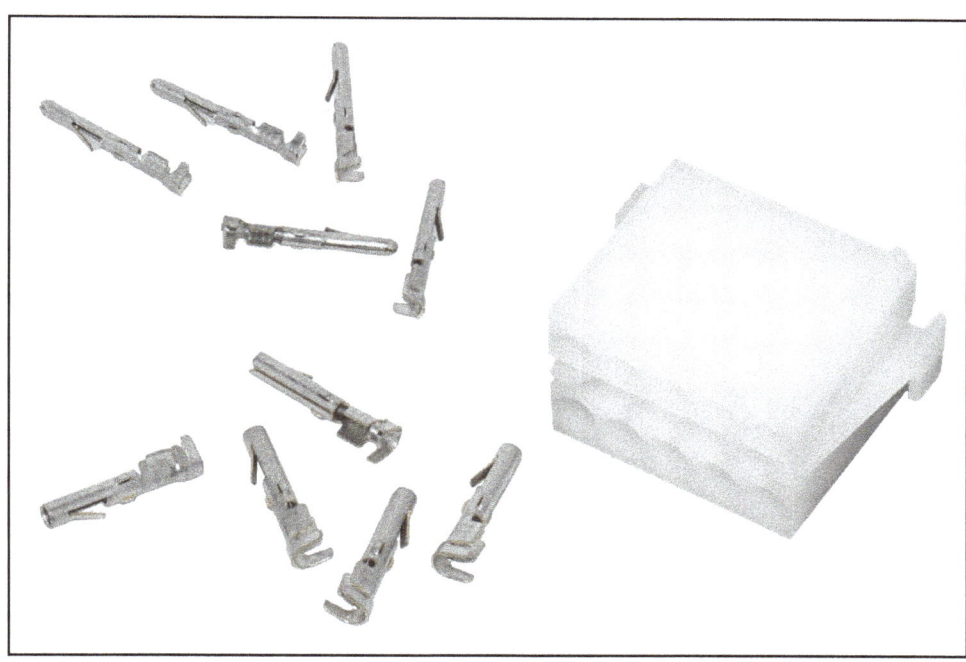

OEM-style Mate-n-Lock connector blocks and pins (used 1971 to 1996) are available in 1 to 12 position male and female connectors and terminals. NAMZ

Did FXRs all run the same wiring harness? If not what are the breakdowns as to the years? And the pros and cons of each harness design?
The FXR started as a Shovelhead with a tapered transmission shaft back in 1982, and the wiring harness used in those first FXRs was used all the way up to the Mid-90's. Those harnesses were associated with AMF and like most of the bikes in this era left much to be desired. The connectors used were an early AMP Mate-n-Lock

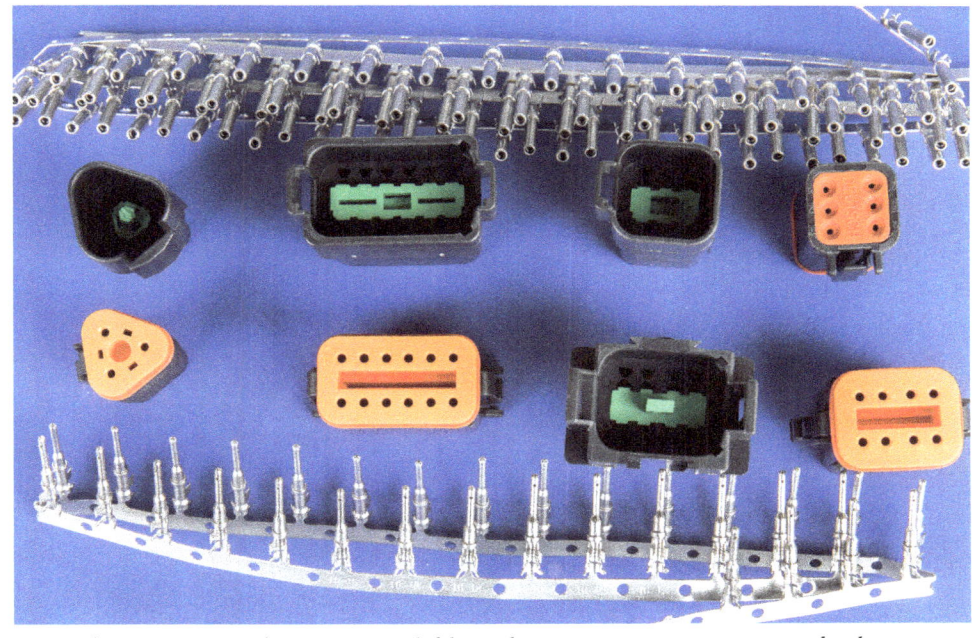

Deutsch connectors and pins are available with 1 to many connectors – multiple connectors and pins are available as kits or most local shops sell individual connectors and pins. These were found at Trask' shop in Phoenix.

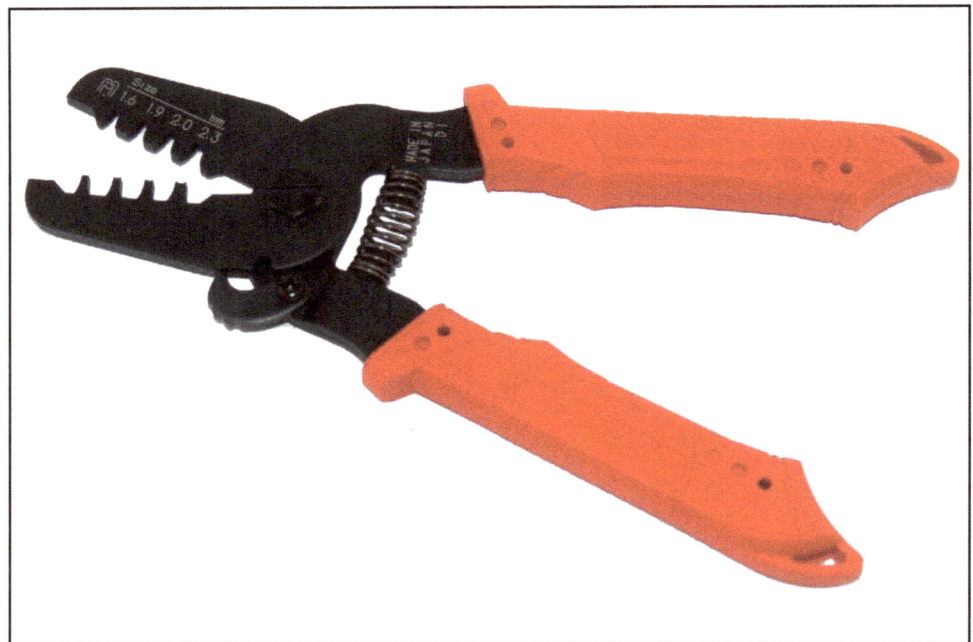

The crimper tool you find at the local auto parts house may not be the best choice when crimping pins for either matenlock or Deutsch. Buy quality. NAMZ

style. They had stamped round male pins and female terminals that didn't make the best contact when taken apart and pushed back together a few times, causing shorts or poor grounds. When the factory needed to tap into a wire, they used a metal "bridge" inside the male connectors that snugly fit around (2) or more terminals at the same time. A simple way to "tap" power or ground, but not ideal by any means. AMP Mate-n-Lock connectors were not watertight and were generally not good fitting connectors. They were VERY hard to de-pin when service or replacement was needed causing many damaged extraction tools or busted knuckles. Most people would just cut them off! Other issues with the wiring on these early models was the wire jacket which seemed to dry out quickly causing it to crack and leave sections of wire without any insulation. These harnesses and connectors went away in 1996 and were replaced by the watertight and easy to service Deutsch DT Series connector family. Unless a pristine 1990's FXR is found, one of the first things I would do with a FXR is rewire the entire bike including the ignition.

Most pins, Mate-n-Lock and Deutsch, require two crimps on each pin – one on the wire and one on the insulation. If the crimps aren't neat (done with the right crimp tool) the pins don't slide in to the connector blocks as designed they may not make a good connection.

Let's talk a little about people who have FXRs, especially the early ones. Can you expand on the electrical problems those owners can expect, and what can they do to minimize electrical issues – short of replacing the entire harness? As mentioned above, early model FXR's or any 1980's Harley Davidsons for that matter, are over 30-years old. They have seen their fair share of weather, abuse, and mechanical neglect. It's pretty safe to say that the wiring harness has been chopped up more than once. Connectors have been cut off; there is a lot of electrical tape, butt-connectors, t-tap slices and maybe even wire nuts. Yes, wire nuts, I've seen it all. The best idea when tackling an older FXR is to come up with a checklist. Start with the motor, transmission, primary, wheels, neck and swingarm bearings, (good luck with those) then replace the motor-mounts. Now check the charging system and battery. Last, investigate the wiring harness. If it looks good and you don't have any issues, leave it alone but I don't think you're going to be so lucky. And consider replacing the ignition. The bike started with a basic dual fire cam position sensor and coil that is controlled by the kill switch. If you're unsure of what you have or it's reliability, I would suggest replacing it with a new single fire version. Also check those battery cables, they are so important. Make sure you have a ground wire from the starter mount to the frame and the frame to the battery – as the motor is rubber mounted and thus insulated from the chassis.

Ok. Now, what about builders who take the bike down to the frame and want to start fresh with a complete harness. Tell us what a person should look for in a harness kit? If it were my project, I would install our complete bike harness, part number NCBH-01-A. This harness gives you everything you need to rewire you bike properly, using Harley color-coded wire, (3) ATO fuses, a full-size starter

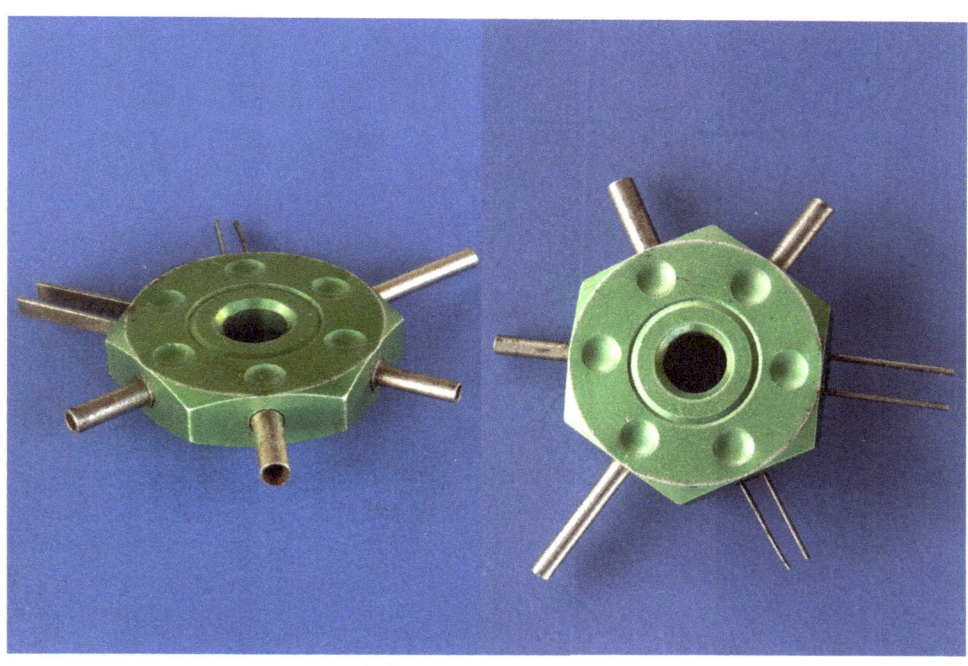

Tools like this are handy to de-pin the pin(s) from the connector block - they're available from a variety of sources (this one is from Snap-On).

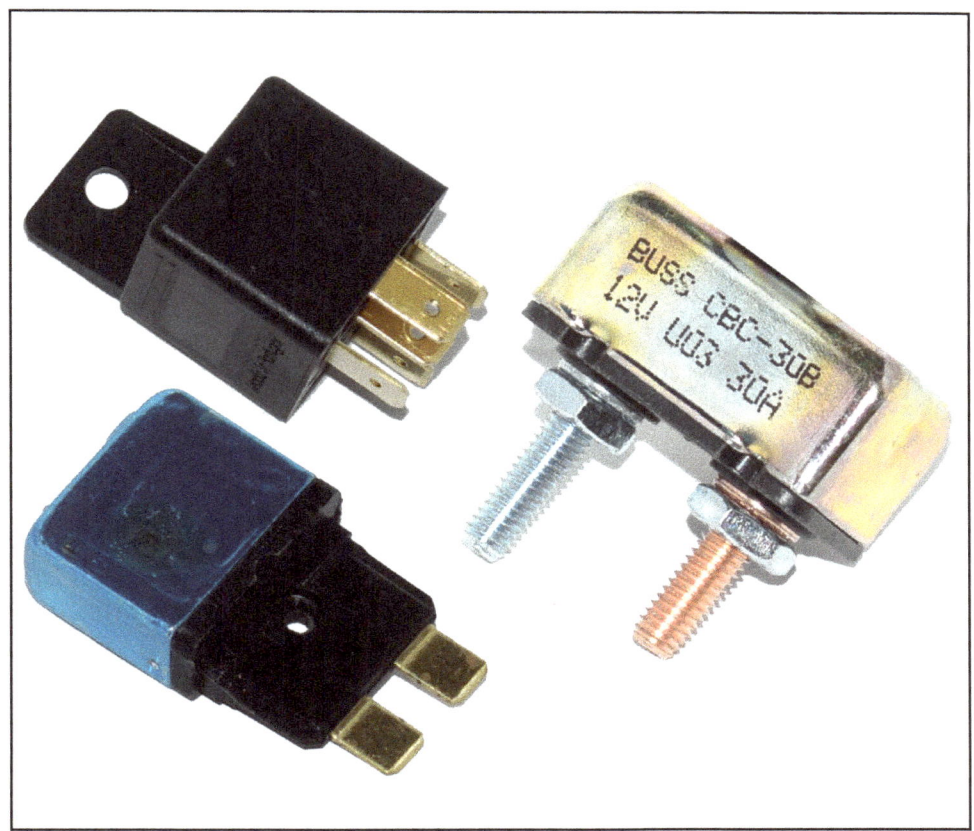

Most Harleys use a starter relay (top left), and many use circuit breakers. Be sure to use the breaker with the correct rating. NAMZ

21

relay, charging circuit breaker and a Badlands Self-Canceling Turn Signal Module. The kit also includes all of the connectors and heat shrink needed to do the job right the first time. Since you bike is torn down, you can drill holes to hide the wiring or clean up the mounting areas for the circuit breakers or OEM ignition module. Most importantly, if you're not sure about the condition or life of the stator, rotor or regulator, REPLACE THEM ALL. Don't take any chances, as it's better to roll it off the lift knowing everything is all new, than to wait for a breakdown.

How much work is it – really – to install the harness. Can a semi-experienced mechanic install the harness and make everything work?
When replacing a complete wiring harness is in order, the best advice is to prepare yourself. It's really not that hard if there's a plan. Make sure you have all of the components and they're operational, or purchase new versions. As I said, be sure the frame is ready to wire, holes are drilled and mounting locations are thought out before going to paint or powder coat.

Decide where the ground wire from the starter base will be bolted onto the frame. Then grind a small circle, about ¼ inch in diameter, where the cable will be bolted to the frame. This will ensure proper continuity. Once you have the frame prepared, you're ready to start wiring. NAMZ offers two after-market styles of complete wiring harnesses, one complete with turn signals (mentioned above) and a bare bones style without turn signal capabilities. These harnesses are universal and will work with ANY Harley Davidson/American, custom V-Twin. They both have all the features and extras mentioned above.

A full color wiring schematic along with the right pre-planning will allow for a perfect installation, even for those with limited experience. You need to have the right tools, the understanding, and patience to do the job right.

If you're not sure of your skill set, ask someone with both knowledge and experience. Don't take make mistakes that could cost you much more than money in the end.

The typical charging system is made up of three components: regulator, stator and rotor. Wise mechanics suggest replacing all three components when there's trouble with one.

Chapter Four

Drivetrain Choices for your FXR

Q&A with Mark Shadley

Tell us a little about Shadley Bros and AutoTec? I was introduced to motorcycles by my father at a very young age. At 13 I started working as a mechanic. I took shop classes in high school, and later I took night classes at a trade school. Between working in the shop and taking classes at night, I learned the trade and the business. During that same period of time, I was always building bikes at night and on weekends.

My brother Paul started pretty young too. When he graduated from high school he came to work with me, and in May of 1981 we officially opened AutoTec for automotive repair and auto body repair. After considering the fact that we were constantly building and repairing motorcycles for ourselves, we decided to add a motorcycle repair shop to the business as well.

About 20 years later we put up a new building. That was 2000. The building was designed to fit all the needs of our growing business. The new building includes an automotive repair area, auto body shop with a state of the art zero-emissions paint booth, a comprehensive motorcycle service area complete with a store, a dyno room, and a fabrication area for custom bike building.

You and Paul have been FXR fans for 25 Years at least. What is it about FXRs that appeals to you two? We like FXRs because they're cool! They handle well, they're lightweight and they lend

If you want serious horsepower for your FXR project, a healthy Twin Cam is the way to go, but as always power comes with a price tag.

Stock FXR frame, ready for paint and the installation of an Evo.

themselves to performance work. When they came out we started using them right away. We just like the way they handle, drive and look.

How do you advise a customer who wants to build a FXR but isn't sure of the drivetrain choice. How do you help that person decide on choosing an Evo or Twin Cam? The Evo motors are a lot easier to install and they take a whole lot less time, energy and effort. The bikes were manufactured with Evos so the Evos are very easy to install. It's far more cost efficient than switching to a Twin Cam - it's a lot less work. The motor-to-transmission setup is the weak link on the Evos. The O-ring lip on the left side case breaks off when the bikes are ridden hard.

The Twin Cam motor has a better, stronger, motor-to-transmission setup. They stay together a lot better than the Evos, and they're capable of big inches with a lot more power than you can get from an Evo. If you want a more powerful motor with less aggravation, you're better off with a Twin Cam.

Stock FXR frame – minus any kickstand bracket and the mid-frame cross-member, modifications necessary for the installation of a Twin Cam with stock oil pan.

What are the major steps necessary to adapt a Twin Cam to a frame originally meant for an Evo? The way that I do it is to remove the braces that run across the bottom of the frame, because the Twin Cam oil pan hits the braces. I move the center brace forward and the back brace all the way back. I do this one brace at a time so none of the frame dimensions change.

Now they make an oil pan that's designed to clear the cross-members. They're expensive, but when you consider someone working at home, it might be easier to just swap out the oil pan rather then bring the frame to a shop to have the work done.

What about putting a wider tire in a FXR factory frame? To put in a 150 or wider wider tire, I start with a narrow belt, I just change out the rear pulley. The narrow belts stand up to hard riding pretty well and you get rid of all the maintenance and mess that comes with a chain. To make room for the tire and the fender I take a belt grinder and open up the inside of the frame. Then I take flat stock and cut careful filler patches and weld them in – I have to do that because I've opened up the tubing with all the grinding. Removing the material and running the narrow belt makes room for a significantly wider tire.

What do you like to use for a swingarm? When I'm doing a twin cam, I use a 2001-2008 swingarm off of a Bagger or I buy an aftermarket swingarm. I do prefer a swingarm that's ¾ of an inch to an inch longer than stock. If you look at most FXRs the center of tire is located forward, not centered under the fender. And the end of the fender is hanging off the end at the back. So the longer swingarm looks better, and it helps when you're doing a hole shot.

What about an aftermarket frame vs. a Harley frame? There is a lot to consider when choosing the frame. The main reason that I like to use the original Harley frame is because you have a title with VIN numbers. You don't have to go through the hassle of titling the bike, which can be a long process. You can build a bike using a aftermarket frame bike, it's easier to build with an aftermarket frame, but it depends on the laws of titling the bike in your state. Sometimes, in strict states, you're better off starting with a factory frame that has a clean title. Buy a clean bike then sell off all of the old parts you're not going to use, you can make some extra money that way.

Are there any other issues related to this that people miss when considering Evo or Twin Cam? Fuel injection or carbureted is a big deal. Fuel injection tunes nice, it's a good way to go, but it's more work. We have done some Twin Cams that have fuel injection, and that really worked out well,

A Twin Cam will fit in a FXR frame, but the fit is tight.

Note the clearance between the motor and frame.

An Evo slides right in – not surprising considering that FXR frames carried Evo power plants for 10+ years.

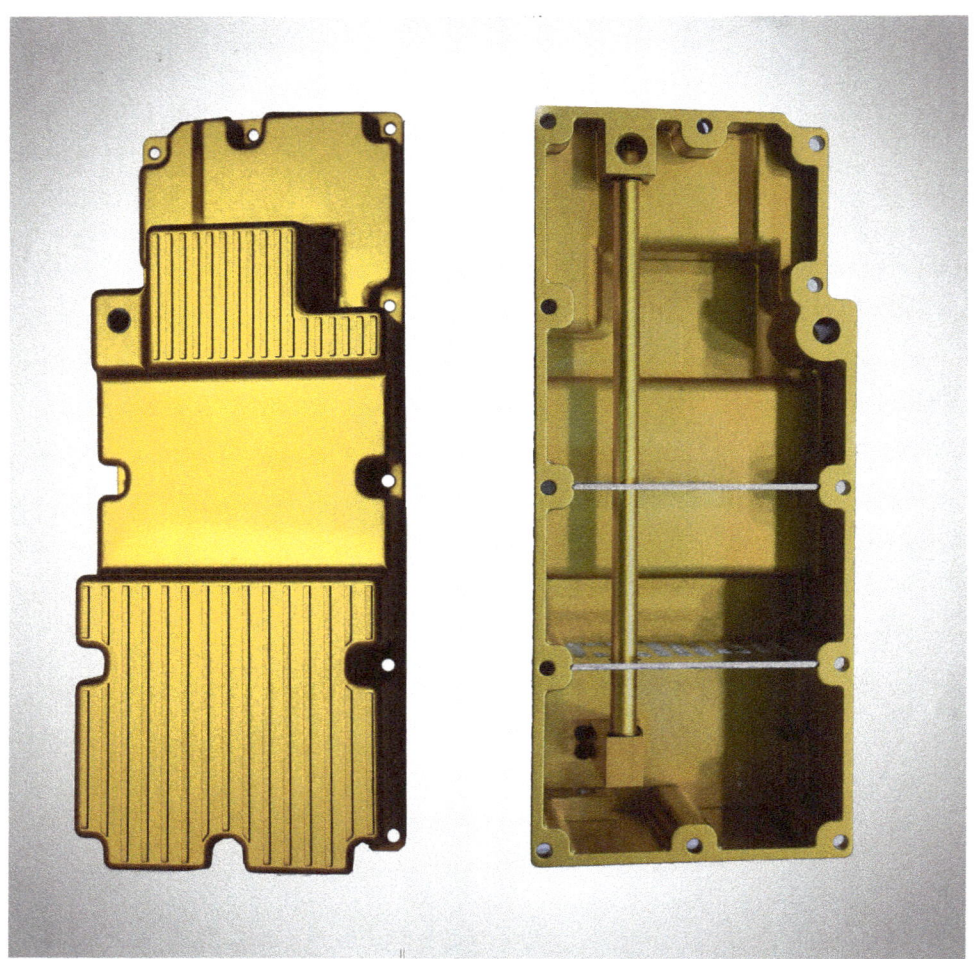

There are two ways to deal with the interference between the Twin Cam oil pan and the frame – cut out and move the cross-member(s), or use an oil pan from Deviant Fabrications.

but you've got to know what you're doing in the electrical field in order to do that.

Do you plan to put an M-8 in FXR Frame?
I do plan to put a M-8 in to an FXR frame when the job and the time comes up. I will definitely put a Milwaukee 8 in to an FXR frame.

Five FXRs, and four Shadley Brothers - yes, the Shadley Bros were early adopters of the FXR platform.

Chapter Five

The Importance of a Clean Title

Q&A with Rob Kenney

Rob: Give us a little background on you; what puts you in a good position to advise bike builders on how to avoid purchasing a bike or frame that likely can't be licensed in their state. I retired in 2018 after 44 years on the Police Force. I have extensive hands-on experience since 1977 in Motorcycle Identification. I wrote the Law-Enforcement-Only Manuals on Harley-Davidson, Sport Bikes, ATV's and Aftermarket V-Twin Identification. I've also worked in the Motorcycle Theft Task Forces around the country (BBB, Daytona, Myrtle Beach, Sturgis, Thunder in the Rockies, Vegas and many more). And have personally recovered over 1,000 stolen motorcycles and assisted other Law Enforcement Officers in the identification and recovery of thousands of other stolen motorcycles.

Let's assume I buy a complete bike on eBay. It's likely out of state, so how do I make sure the title is legal, that I will be able to title it in my home state? The first thing you need to know - who manufactured the frame? Original factory frames will have a VIN (Vehicle Identification

One of the nice things about a crate motor from a known engine manufacturer is the fact that the motor comes with an MSO, and a receipt from a respected company. This 155 is from R&R Cycles.

Number). All VINs since 1981 are made up of numbers and letters, which are referred to as characters. If it's a Harley frame, it will have a VIN with 17 characters and will always start with "1HD". In the case of Harley-Davidson FXRs, they were manufactured from 1982 through 1994. They were then manufactured as the first CVOs in 1999 (FXR-2 and FXR-3) and 2000 (FXR-4) as limited edition Custom Vehicle Operation motorcycles. The 1982 and 1983 models had 80 CI Shovelhead Engines and all of the 1984 to 2000 models had 80 CI Evolution Engines. All Harley-Davidson FXR VINs begin with "1HD1E".

MANUFACTURERS' CERTIFICATE OF ORIGIN

-MOTORCYCLE FRAMES-

The undersigned MANUFACTURER hereby certifies that the new Motorcycle Frame described below, is the property of said MANUFACTURER, and is transferred this

23 day of February of 2015 on Invoice Number 505425 to

DONNIE SMITH CUSTOM CYCLE

whose address is   10594 RADISSON RD NE
                    BLAINE MN 55449

Shipping Weight 60 pounds   Length in Inches 51

Type of Frame   * S/L CHOP 2 1/4 X 40 ST5

Serial Number   PA1RL1E29FN140045

The MANUFACTURER certifies the above statements are true and correct and that this was the first such new motorcycle frame in trade and commerce.

Executed on 03/16/15 at Carson City, Nevada

Names of Manufacturer   PAUGHCO, INC.

Signature _____   CLERK
                                      Title

Manufacturer's Address   30 COWEE DRIVE
                          P.O. BOX 21390
                          CARSON CITY, NV 89721-1390

SUBSCRIBED and SWORN to before me this

11 day of March, 2015.

NOTARY PUBLIC, NEVADA

Aftermarket frames and motors should come with a MSO, be sure they're filled out correctly so you don't have any trouble when you go to the state to get you title and plates.

How about the numbers on aftermarket frames, how do I judge those? Aftermarket frames should have a Frame Identification Number, it is NOT a VIN and can have any number of characters and would begin with any characters. Most of the frame manufacturers do use a 17 character Frame Identification Number. All these frames came with an MSO when new, but require a Bill of Sale if used. The most common FXR aftermarket frames use an Identification Number that starts with:

1A9HS74A – Atlas Frames from California (Out of Business). 1B91 - Jammer Frame from California (Out of Business (OOB). 1D9SS64D – Daytec from California (OOB). 1RC10, 1RC11 or 1RC14 – Rowe Frame from New Hampshire (OOB). 1SD or SUN - Sundance from Florida (OOB). 1WA5FX or 1WE5FX – Wildcat Frames (OOB). 2MXC, 2MMW or MMWS – Maximum Metalworks from Canada (OOB). 2RTMC072 – Rolling Thunder of Canada, believed to be in limited business. 2T91FGL – Tripoli from Canada (OOB). 4B7H8469 – Santee from California believed to still be in business. 4EM or PA1 – Paughco from Nevada, still in Business. 4K7S8135 – Kraft-Tech from California, believed to still be in business. PRO –

Kenny Boyce from California, believed to be OOB, The Frame Identification Number could be 7 to 9 characters or 17 characters. Chopper Guys from California (believed to be out of business) frame identification numbers can start with 2 numbers or a letter and number followed by CGX for FXR Frames. I.E.: 95CGX or B7CGX.

There are dozens of other Frame Manufacturers that are no longer in business and may have made a few FXR frames that are not listed.

How can I check a frame or bike to insure it wasn't stolen or was issued a salvaged vehicle? There is a website that it available to the public, maintained by the National Insurance Crime Bureau (NICB). At this site, you can enter the VIN and it will show you if it is reported as stolen or listed as salvage. The site's address is: NICB.ORG, then go to the box with VIN CHECK and enter the VIN. It is very simple and easy to use. This will save you lots of time and worry. I suggest that you print the page with the results to keep in your build folder in case an issue ever arises about the VIN of your bike.

What about suggestions regarding the paperwork required by most states to license a built-bike with a minimal amount of hassle. As far as what paperwork that is required or suggested for each State, that is a hard question to answer - each state is different. My suggestion is to have as much complete paperwork as possible (and it's a good idea to keep back-up copies). You should always have Bills of Sale or receipts for all of the major components of a built motorcycle. This would include the frame, engine, transmission, front-end, wheels and tires. Also, sheet metal: gas tank(s), fenders and electrical system. As far as engines, an MSO or Bill of Sale for bare engine cases is probably not sufficient. You should have receipts for the complete engine or all of the components that were used to build the engine.

The receipts should include a Bill or Sale and Title if it is an original Harley-Davidson Frame.

The risk in buying a used engine is the missing MSO, and questions regarding the origin of the motor.

Some States might have incorrectly registered a motorcycle as a Harley-Davidson - with an Aftermarket Frame Number. This is wrong, but is not uncommon. Also, some states, like Florida, will cancel any registration found listed as a Harley-Davidson with an Aftermarket Frame Identification Number or non Harley-Davidson VIN. Your receipts should also include a Bill of Sale for the engine. If the engine (or cases) you're using is from a complete Harley-Davidson motorcycle, you should include a copy of the title where the engine (or cases) originated (if possible). Keep a copy or Bill of Sale and/or title copy for your build folder, in case that motorcycle is later stolen and the engine you have now comes back as stolen.

Any final words of wisdom? Just remember what's been said already: have as much complete paperwork as possible when you go in to register the bike.

A, B, Cs of Motorcycle Insurance

Q&A Hank Ham

Hank: Can you tell us how long you've been in the vehicle insurance business? And how long you've been a motorcycle rider? I've been in the insurance business since 1985. I had my first bike when I was 10 years old, a Honda 100 Dirt bike. My last dirt bike, 40 years later, took me south to run the Baha 500, it kicked my ass. My first H-D, was a 87 FXR, and I still have that bike, (the best bike the MoCo ever built). I've built several bikes from scratch, which ended up as centerfold pieces, good luck I suppose. In addition to the customs I have a couple of bikes that I bought off the rack.

If I walk into your office with the title of my new bike that I built from an aftermarket frame, can you find me good insurance at a reasonable price? Good insurance... most likely. Reasonable, all depending on how savvy your insurance agent is. There's a hand full of insurance companies that will insure a builder bike, show them the pictures, list high-end components.

Insurance revolves around safety for you the consumer, and getting what you want. If your bike is stolen, you want your insurance carrier to give you enough money to buy the same year, make, and model Nothing more, nothing less. PS, if you have a nice paint job, custom wheels, tons of go fast parts. Tell your insurance agent. The basic policy usually does NOT include coverage for most bolt-on parts.

Production bikes have a ton of safety measures to keep the riders safe, the builder-bike much less so, which scares the insurance carrier enough to decline insurance for builder bikes that don't have a 17 digit VIN, or a title that says "home made."

> **If you have a nice paint job, custom wheels, tons of go-fast parts, tell your insurance agent. The basic policy usually does NOT include coverage for most bolt-on parts.**

Another issue with bikes built from scratch is, if there's an accident caused by the builder you have no recourse. When a production bike goes wrong, due to the manufacturer or/dealer, they have a ton of product liability, which means there's money to fix or replace the bike, not to mention funds for injured riders. That is not the case for a bike built in your garage.

Are there any red flags that sometimes come up in this situation? Things about the bike or the paperwork that make it more difficult to get good insurance? Get good pictures, list the components used. If you had help from a motorcycle shop, get them to provide a detailed listing of parts and accessories.

Chapter Six

The FXR Shows

Joe Mielke

Joe, how about a little background on you. Some of us know you from your years at Klock Werks and the sheet metal posts, can you expand on that a little and bring us up to date. Also, I understand you've just moved to Sturgis - congratulations you live where most of the readers would like to live – how does the move dove tail with your efforts to promote and support the FXR and Dyna models?

Well in high school I was a car guy before motorcycles were even on my radar. I got my first motorcycle at 18 because mom told me I couldn't have one. Ha ha! When I first started riding I was into sport bikes and didn't care much for Harleys. We're talkin' the early 90s and most of what you saw being customized were Harley FXRs so they were still something I was interested in. Fast forward a lot of years and I'm working at Klock Werks. I was there for close to 12 years. I started behind the parts counter and was designer/project coordinator/lead fabricator when I left. The first few years of the FXR Show happened while employed and have continued since. My main focus to earn a living since starting my own business (Snap Fabrications) has been custom metal shaping and metal shaping tools.

My move to Sturgis is an effort to grow my business and to try and re-establish myself in the motorcycle world. A divorce changed my life and pulled my focus from what I'm good at. So I needed a shock to my system. Hence the move to Sturgis. I'm certain more things will come from my move

Looking down on the turnout at the Chip. As Joe says, not too bad for a show that celebrates two obsolete models.

and tie into the FXR Show and my involvement with events during the Sturgis Rally. I've always wanted to live in the black hills region so I'm excited about that for sure.

What was the year for the first FXR show in Sturgis? And can you give us a few details, the location and how many bikes turned up for the inaugural show?

The first year was 2013 in Sturgis City Park. It was the first motorcycle event allowed in City Park since the infamous "out house fire" got the rally banned from City Park. I'm pretty proud to be able to say that. To have an idea if anyone would actually come to an FXR only show I did a pre-registration. I had over 20 pre-register. I figured if I had 20 show up that would be a success. We had 60 FXRs show that first year.

Did you include the Dyna from the very beginning?

I didn't include the DYNA platform until 2016. By that time the lines between custom FXRs and custom Dynas had become blurred and more and more Dyna riders wanted to bring their bikes to the show. We were also coming off the 75th rally and I wanted to make sure the show would grow after an anniversary year. Typically attendance at the rally goes down after an anniversary year. So I added the "Dyna Mixer" part of the show.

When you announced the first FXR show, FXRs weren't all that popular – a lot of people didn't even know what a FXR was. So, what gave you the idea to hold a show for a somewhat obscure and obsolete Harley model?

I had been searching for an FXR for a few years and found one I liked at Black Hills Harley during the Sturgis Rally in 2012 and purchased it. I made it my own and rode as much as I could the rest of 2012, as weather would permit. Winter came and I wasn't riding. But when the streets were clear I'd ride even if it was cold. I live in South Dakota so you can figure that out. New Year 2013 I decided to make a New Years resolution to ride every Friday for a year, Rain or Shine. I started FXR Friday and shared my rides on my social media.

They sometimes call him Big Joe, the man who organizes the shows and puts out any small fires that erupt during a show.

Twin Cam power, two-into-one exhaust, inverted forks, high-end rear shocks – all becoming standard issue on current FXRs.

I rode a lot in the cold and on the snow. My FXR ended up with knobby tires and ice-racing studs. I took the FXR everywhere it was never intended to go. After several months of FXR Friday's on social media I was getting a bunch of messages from other FXR owners telling me about the love they have for the FXR platform. I could see there was something to it so I started asking if there would be interest in an FXR only bike show at Sturgis and made it happen. I ended up riding every FXR Friday for a year and a half before missing a Friday because I was on the road and didn't have an FXR to ride. It was a good run!

How did the shows evolve over the next few years, you went from the Sturgis Park to a gravel parking lot, and eventually to the Cross Roads at the Chip. How did you end up at the Chip, and were there times along the way when you wondered if it was all worth it, the work and the organizing?

Well, I really enjoyed hosting the show at City Park. For the Sturgis Rally 75th anniversary the City of Sturgis allowed all of city park to be used for rally week events. It didn't turn out so well for the promoter or the City of Sturgis. My FXR Show was great however. That was the first year that we had over 100 FXRs in the show. Unfortunately there was a lot of backlash from the community after that week of events. The year after I went back to the city to make sure I was still good to host my show the way I had previous to the mess of the 75th. They told me no. There was a new rally director that year and he told me I needed to go to city council meetings to plead my case and I would probably need to circulate a petition to show the Sturgis community supported my show. I didn't have that kind of time so I walked away. I thought about not doing the show any more. I looked at other possible venues. Time was running out to put the show together for 2016. Glencoe campground offered up some space near the Sturgis Dragway. The gravel lot you mentioned. I thought the tie-in with the dragway would be fun. I think everyone still had fun but it was a bit of a disaster from my perspective. Everything was last minute but we made it happen. Leading up to the next year I had some communications with the Buffalo Chip about taking the show to the Crossroads venue. My wife at the time and I went to the Chip and met with Woody and his staff to make the arrangements for the 2017 Sturgis Rally. It all looked good. About a month later my wife left me. I was gutted,

As the shows have grown, so has support from the aftermarket companies like Brock's Performance, displaying their Carbon wheels and chassis components for FXRs and Dynas.

Perhaps the best thing about the shows is not only the success, but the variety of motorcycles that show – from cruisers to highway haulers to drag race machines.

No two FXRs are the same, could this one be a Billy Westbrook creation?

No matter whether it's a RT or Dyna or stripped FXR, there is one thing they all have in common. These are bikes that are ridden, used and occasionally abused.

No custom bike show would be complete without the awards ceremony at the end.

Shovel power, factory wheels and sheet metal, a nice early FXR.

Looking across the grounds during one of the FXR shows, it's hard to believe that when the FXRT models came out everyone swore they were; "ugly and too Japanese."

More FXRTs, at least two with aftermarket fairings – available now from a number of manufacturers.

I didn't know up from down. I walked away from anything I was involved in. Including my business, the Hamsters and the FXR Show. Fortunately with the support of the Buffalo Chip, Marilyn Stemp and some great volunteers the FXR Show still happened that year. After getting my mind right I came back to run the show in 2018 to continue to grow the show at its home at the Buffalo Chip. We had continued success in 2019 and look forward to the 80th anniversary for the Sturgis Rally in 2020.

The 2019 show seemed to be well attended. How many bikes did you have? And have you experienced growth not only in the number of bikes that attend, but in the support from the aftermarket, and from enthusiasts who aren't necessarily FXR or Dyna riders?

2019 was good. We had approximately 100 FXRs and 20 Dynas. The last three years have had an attendance of somewhere between 120-130 total motorcycles. Not bad for two obsolete models of motorcycles. I'm fortunate to have a lot of friends in the industry. I believe I have a good reputation as well, which has always provided me with ample support for the show. Several manufacturers have been sponsors every year since the beginning. I do have volunteers who are not FXR or Dyna owners and we certainly have people attend who are not owners either. The idea for the show was to get people together at a bike show to talk bikes and tell stories. No egos, hang-ups and nobody worries about winning a crappy trophy. It's about the people and their common bond. The second part of show has always been that it's a charity fundraiser. It started as a way for me to be able to give a sizable donation to Children's Care Hospital and School of SD. We continue to raise money for the same organization which is now called LifeScape.

What are your plans for the shows over the next few years? And do you have plans for shows or FXR events of a different sort?

Not much as far as plans will change for 2020. The format will most likely remain the same until rider/owners lose interest. The FXR will always be cool but trends always change. The only new show idea right now is an EVO only show. It's Marilyn Stemp's brainchild and I'm going to help her make it happen. Should be fun!

Joe can be contacted regarding the next FXR/Dyna show at: Joe@fxrshow.com

Volunteers run the show, and there are plenty to help you find the best parking spot. Profits go to LifeScape, a South Dakota charity for children.

In most custom bike circles low means cool. For most FXR riders, low means (too) slow – in the curves.

Chapter Seven

Planning

The Forgotten Step

If you really want to *build* a custom motorcycle, then there's one step that's more important than the parts you buy. Planning. Yes, you can simply bolt parts onto that frame on your hoist, and then stand back in pride after each installation. All too often, however, building a bike piece by piece results in a custom that isn't really a custom, just a dressed up stocker. What you're added is what "Tank" (Ron Ewsichek) used to call, lipstick and high heels.

Not only have you missed the target, you likely spent more money to get less, because in hindsight you will realize that some of the parts don't fit the theme and don't play well with the others. So, let's go back to the very beginning.

What'a ya want

What do you really want? A bare bones simple stop-light hot rod like Neil Ryan's red FXR seen in the Gallery? Or do you want a road machine built from nothing but the best equipment, like Lars' bright yellow and black FXRT with Twin Cam power?

Lowered, with a nice paint job and a Café fairing – Jason's bike is a good example of the notion that sometimes less is more.

Now back up two more steps and consider, first, how you intend to use the machine. Consider whether this will it be a second bike, or your daily ride?

Next, decide what you have for a budget. A kick ass Twin Cam will surely look good sitting in that frame and literally kick your ass down the street, but it will take more green (and time) than a mild Evo.

Once you're thought long and hard about how the new ride is likely to be used, and how much money is in the coffee can, you can start working on the design – and compiling the lists.

Any kind of serious work on your motorcycle requires a true hoist, one that gets the bike well off the ground and leaves some extra real estate for tools and parts.

Aesthetics

If there's a bike or two that really appeals to you, collect some photos and identify what it is that you like about those bikes, is it the way they sit, the paint job, the way the fairing is mounted?

Power and Chassis

We've said it before; installing a Twin Cam in your FXR will likely cost more than an Evo. For the extra money you get more cubes and more potential horsepower. They also give the bike a different look, a more modern vibe. And if you're dealing with a factory FXR chassis then that modern vibe will require modification to the frame or the oil pan.

An aftermarket FXR frame is a bit like a Twin Cam, in the sense that there are numerous advantages, but they come with a price tag. If you want to

Seen at one of the shows, this Twin Cam rocket is breaking new ground aesthetically.

Orange Crush is another creation of Kurt at Lil' Evil. Color is candy tangerine (an H-D color) but painted over a gold base to create a very nice orange. Power comes from a hot rod Evo.

run a wide tire, or need more rake, run a Twin Cam without cutting and fabricating, then the extra cash may be well spent – especially if you're starting from scratch instead of working on a FXR you already own. Beware the trade-offs however, that come with the aftermarket frame, as noted in chapter 05.

Chassis component choices include things like the front fork, the rear shocks, and even the swingarm. Upside-down fork assemblies are definitively catching on in the V-twin market. You can buy a complete assembly from Storz Performance or look on eBay for a 'Busa fork assembly – installed with aftermarket triple trees available from Brock's. If you keep the stock forks, there are a variety of kits to improve their performance and/or change the length.

In back you have to choose between the shocks that came with the bike, or a pair of shocks from a supplier like Drag Specialties. If you want the bike to sit lower, or higher, than stock, then for sure you're going to be shopping for new shocks in the appropriate length.

In the End

Now you've put together a folder, either a paper one or an electrical model. Listed are the photos of bikes you lust over, useful for picking the ideal paint job and overall look. Once you have the overall look, you can pick

Installing an inverted fork in a FXR or Dyna is relatively easy, thanks to Brock's for their triple trees (and tube extensions too).

the ideal parts necessary to achieve that visual. And you've decided how the bike will be used, another choice among many, that needs to be determined prior to buying parts. To the right of the Ohlins shocks or the wheels from Drag or Brock's, that lists the price. Don't forget labor charges for things like paint, and possible help with things like wiring or welding, which may be skills outside of your wheelhouse.

For anyone who started with a complete FXR, there's also a "plus" column The list of stock parts that you don't plan to use, which means you can sell them on eBay or at the local swap meet – and offset the cost of the new shocks, the paint job and all the rest.

The TV shows were full of videos with bike builders competing against each other, or the clock, or both. In our own small garages it's easy to get caught up in a deadline – be it Sturgis or a particular annual bike show. While the deadline helps ensure that the bike will get finished instead of languishing in the shop, it can also be the enemy.

Knowledgeable builders often set the rolling chassis on the hoist and then use simple templates cut from light board or even particleboard, to determine which tank, or bag or even fender will "work" the best. The same individuals leave the template in place for a few days and then spend a few minutes each day standing back and simply looking at the bike. If your shop is small, it's even a good idea to roll the project out onto the driveway so you and get far enough away to really ascertain whether or not a certain component has the right shape and works

This 1982 Shovel is the work of J. Waggaman, who modified the rear frame to eliminate the struts, rolled the edge of the fender, added rake to the neck, and installed a wide glide fork. Clean to the max.

Lauri's 1993 FXR is another mild custom… just slam 'em, dress up the paint, use mini turn signals, angle the license plate and replace the stock taillight. Oh yea, and replace those ugly seats.

Some of us are never satisfied. Crazy John stuffed a 145 into this FXR frame, and hung a NOS bottle on the other side. With the stock rear tire shown here it became an exhibition machine – instant smoke - forcing John to install a slick at a later date.

with the rest of the design. Extra fenders and tanks, borrowed from friends or found at a swap meet, are also handy. Don't assume a certain front fender is the best. Hang a few other options between the fork legs and then stand back.

Not every FXR project is complex enough to justify following all the suggestions made above. The point though is worth repeating. It's too easy to install the wrong shocks or mount a fender so it rubs the tire at high speed or on a big bump – and not find the mistake until after the bike is finished and on the road.

Think first. That's all. Just think.

A painter by trade, Brian's bike is all about the paint and finish (note the before pic). "I messed with the formula for the candy orange, and sprayed it over an orange base. The air cleaner, most covers and pushrod tubes are a copper color, the engine and tranny case are one shade darker."

Chapter Eight

How It All Started

By Bill Radcliffe

1983 FXR

This started as I was trying to pick a gift for my fiancé's birthday. The second bike Colleen owned was an Evo FXR. When I asked her if she would want another FXR - one like the bike she had so much fun on - she thought yes, it would be fun. She didn't, however, want another Evo. Instead she wanted an original Shovelhead since so few were made. We also felt it was important to find a stock, clean, original FXR, one that would make a nice addition to our small collection of classic bikes.

Our new 1983 FXR came from the original owner with 7250 miles on the odometer. The only things that weren't stock were the solo seat (we have the original) and the pipes. Otherwise the bike came with all the original features and in excellent condition. It runs perfect and shows well. Well enough to win awards in the original category at several bike shows. It's so close to bone stock that people in the know always want to buy our FXR. But the answer is no, it's definitely not for sale.

Hard to find, a stock 1983 FXR, complete with the factory air cleaner. Not perfect perhaps, given the pipes and seat, but very close and easily converted to a 100% stock FXR.

Stock Shovelhead, 80 cubic inches fed by a Bendix carburetor. Note the aluminum heads and dark, cast iron cylinders.

Eyebrow over the headlight was there from the beginning. Early examples came with 35mm fork tubes.

Solo seat is not standard, Bill has the original seat in the garage.

A simple machine - no ABS, digital gauges or information screen with GPS. Just a motor and tranny with primary, two wheels, tires and brakes, a few lights. What else does a person need?

I don't think this Shovel will be turning 8,000 rpms any time soon. Odometer read just over 7,000 miles when purchased by the current owners.

If you're going to have a gas gauge you have to have a dash.

Chapter Nine

A New/Old Luxury Liner

Arlen's Dream

When Arlen Ness dreamed up his Luxury Liner – based on his tried and true "FXR" frame - he likely never dreamed that decades in the future someone would take the bones of his design and create a new motorcycle. One that's as modern as a bike can be while still paying homage to the appeal of the original.

It all started when Mark Shadley bought a certain basket case. This one wasn't an old Pan or Shovel with the parts spread out into a dozen greasy cardboard boxes. No, this basket case included nearly everything a person would need to build a genuine Luxury Liner. As Mark explains: "I purchased the basket from a guy who bought the parts he needed to build a Ness Luxury Liner, back in the day. He had the frame, fairing, Ness bags, everything, even a complete motor and transmission. But he never assembled the bike."

"A friend of mine, Bobby Gerone, heard about the kit and bought it from me. Then he turned around and suggested that I reassemble the basket into a runner. But, he didn't want just a perfect 'Liner, he wanted more, something a little more current."

Reinventing an Arlen Ness Luxury Liner is a little like customizing a Ferrari. The craftsman needs to bring the machine into the modern world, while retaining the look, appeal and integrity of the original design.

Bobby Garone left most of the details to Mark, though he did have a few must-haves. Like the bags, "Bobby didn't want those early Ness bags," explained Mark. "He wanted modern Bagger bags. And that meant making major changes to the frame. Actually, the back of the bike was the most time consuming part of this build."

With the frame strapped down on the lift, Mark cut off the rear half of the Luxury Liner frame. Then, in order to ensure he could use late model bags and all the rest, he welded on the bolt-on sub-frame used on '09 and later Harley Baggers.

The Shadley shop has an upper shop set aside for the custom builds, so big jobs don't get in the way of day to day work on cars and motorcycles.

To hang modern bags on the bike meant adapting a subframe, used on 2009 and later Baggers, to the Ness machine. Rear fender is from RWD (also the front fender).

Even with the new rear section Mark was still faced with a lot of work on the back of the bike. Like fabricating the bag supports, and modifying the Wernimont rear fender to fit - and making the license plate and taillight mounts integral parts of the fender.

The bags themselves are Down and Out bags from the current Ness catalog, topped with Bad Dad covers – which include built in speakers and some very cool turn signals. With the back of the bike mostly sorted out, Mark could move ahead, literally. The gas tank was another part of the puzzle that turned into a project all its own.

"It came with a gas tank," explains Mark, "but it sat up way too high, and I couldn't mount it any lower because the bottom of the tank would hit the rocker boxes. So I had to cut the bottom out and make a new bottom and tunnel. After welding it all together with the new mounts, it sat nice and low on the bike."

Creating the just-right silhouette for this custom required more than just a re-manufactured tank. As Mark explains the process, "I lowered the fairing on the frame, and changed the radius just behind the front fender. I also trimmed some material on the lower parts of the fairing." Part of massaging the Ness fairing included the creation of a new dash that wrapped across the top of the fairing. The new dash was designed to accept the very modern digital multi-reading gauge from Motogadget.

With the various body parts and sheet metal

Bags are typical late model Bagger items from the current Ness catalog, with lids from Bad Dad - note the integral turn signals.

The tank came with the Ness-kit, but required serious surgery before it would sit low on the frame and look like it belongs there.

The Ness-kit came with a stock 96 inch S&S engine - only 2 changes - rounded cylinders and diamond cut cylinders and heads. Covers are Boyd/Perewitz items from back in the day.

modified and massaged, it was time to think about the drivetrain. The V-Twin that came with all the rest of the basket wasn't just any motor, but a complete and never-run 96-inch engine from S&S. "We only made a few changes," explains Mark, "I rounded the cylinders and diamond-cut the fins on the cylinders and heads. And Jim Dorgan in our shop ported the heads. The color on the engine components is something new for us, we used a Cerakote in place of paint or powder coat."

The transmission that came with everything else was typical for the period and contained a five-speed gearset. Given the fact that the new Ness machine could easily reach into triple digits on the highway, a six-speed gear-set was installed.

Smaller bits and pieces that came with everything else included a cam cover and transmission covers, all of them from the short-lived partnership of Bobby Sullivan and David Perewitz.

If there's one truly modern feature on this new customized custom it's the carbon fiber wheels from Brock's Performance – part of a technological revolution that wasn't even a twinkle in Arlen's eye when he designed the Luxury Liner. The width of the wheels required something wider than the narrow fork assembly that came with the kit. Mark chose to install a fork made up of 2013 FLH legs, equipped with Race Tech springs, mounted in triple trees from Sullivan/Perewitz.

The fork legs came complete with Brembo, four-piston calipers. Mark explains that he "smoothed" them out (no H-D logo) and used huge 14-inch rotors from Ness. In back a PM caliper is matched up with a smaller rotor from the same company.

When Arlen designed the Liner chrome was king. Today it's flat paint that's f-ing cool. Once the drive

The Luxury Liner rolls on Carbon wheels from Brock's. Paint colors are a custom mix, with a flattening clear – flat is the new chrome.

train components were coated with flat Cerakote, it seemed only logical to continue the same look throughout the bike.

The paint used on the rest of the bike looks at first like flat primer. The two colors that Mark calls gunmetal, and bronze, were mixed from PPG materials in-house. Credit for the mixing and the application of the paint goes to the Shadley body-shop crew, specifically; Downhill Johnny and California Jim. The graphics were laid out and sprayed by local legend John Hartnet. When it was finished all the components were coated with clear mixed with a flattening agent.

The "51" logo on the bags is a very personal touch, suggested by Bobby Garone and executed in the Shadley Bros. shop. The story goes like this:

Starting with Bobby Garone, 51 was his number when he played football in both high school and college. His father's jersey carried the same number when he played in high school. Bobby's oldest son, Bobby Jr., displayed the family number when he played football in both junior and high school. Finally, the younger son, Nick, wore the number during high school play, and currently displays it on his college jersey.

Given the fact that Mark Shadley didn't just customize a bike, he virtually built one from scratch, a lengthy road test seemed a good idea. "I've built and ridden numerous bikes much like this one," says Mark. "Bikes with similar frames and similar dimensions, so when I took it out on the road, I didn't expect any surprises. What did surprise me was the effect of those Carbon Fiber wheels. The bike works so much better than all those earlier bikes. Going into the turns, it's amazing, it turns-in and rides like a Sportster, even with the 38-degree neck and 5-inches of stretch in the frame. I was amazed so much it really knocked my socks off.

It makes the bike feel so light. I like the bike, but I love those wheels."

Builder	Shadley Bros.
Year/model	2019 Custom FXR
Engine, year, displ.	96 cu. In.
Engine builder	Mark Shadley
Cases	S&S
Cylinders	S&S
Heads	S&S, Jim Dorgan
Aircleaner	S&S
Exhaust	D&D, Mark Shadley
Transmission	Ultima 6-Speed
Frame, stretch/rake	Ness, 5 in., 38 deg
Fork Ass'm	H-D 2015
Triple trees	Custom
Shocks	H-D
Front wheel/tire	Brock's 21X3, Michelin, 120/70-21
Rear wheel/tire	Brock's 18X5, Michelin, 180/55-18
Calipers	PM
Sheet metal	Ness, Shadley Bros.
Sheet metal mods	Shadley Bros.
Painter	Cali & Jim @ Shadley's, John Hartnet grphx
Paint brand	PPG

While the handlebar controls are tried and true items from H-D ("because they work") from Harley-Davidson, the "dash cluster, is a very modern digital component from Motogadget.

Chapter Ten

A Donnie Smith FXR

Hard to believe, but well-known customizer Donnie Smith has owned more than one FXR. It all started with an early model, a 1982 FXR complete with a Shovelhead for power. "I did a trade with a guy and ended up with a FXR," says Donnie. "We didn't do a lot to that bike, I bought short shocks for the back and shorter forks for the front end. Then we added a Mustang seat and a set of drag bars. The bike turned out pretty nice for not much work, and I decided to take it to Sturgis that year (1983) as an extra ride. Well, it turned out I rode that bike most of the week and the more I rode it the more I enjoyed it. The bike had plenty of power, and the ratios in the five-speed were right on. It was just a nice bike to ride."

It turned out that Donnie wasn't the only one who liked the slammed FXR. "I ran into Willie G. during the week," recalls Donnie. "And two years later they brought out the FXR Low Rider. Arlen and David Perewitz saw the FXR and they liked it too. I think that bike helped to establish the FXR as a cool bike – and a good one to customize."

Fast forward to Donnie's most recent FXR – another bike that ended up in Donnie's garage

If Donnie Smith is known for one thing, it's bikes that are elegant rather than radical.

mostly by accident. "I drove up to St. Cloud, MN to do an estimate for a damaged FXR," explains Donnie. "The guy who owned it had already received a check from the insurance company and it turned out that what he really wanted was to sell the bike. So I made him a real low-ball offer, and the bike came home in the back of my van."

"He told me the frame was bent, but after disassembling the bike back at my shop it turned out the frame was OK. My first thought was to just fix what was needed and then flip the bike. But this was about five years ago and FXRs were getting popular again, partly because of the efforts of Joe Mielke and the FXR shows during Sturgis."

In the shop waiting for paint. The grey is Galaxy Grey from H of K, applied by Lenni at Krazy Kolors. Before paint there's always the molding and prep, done by Donnie's brother Greg.

Long and lean – thanks to a subtle stretch on both ends (an extra 1-1/2 inches in both the top tube and the swingarm) and the 35 degree rake.

The FXR that Donnie brought home as a "repairable" came with some nice upgrades, like a chrome tranny case and a chrome front end. The engine was in good condition as well, what people used to call a hot-rod-80.

"Once I decided to keep the bike, I also decided to try a series of changes I wanted to try back in the day," explains Donnie. "We raked the frame to 35 degrees, and lengthened it an inch and a half. We also stretched the swingarm an inch and a half."

Sheet metal changes include a tank two and a half inches longer than stock. The tank-tails arch down to blend with the panels that fill the triangular area under the seat. When Rob Roehl, Donnie's ace tin-man, created the under seat

Simple and ultra clean. Fabricated handlebars, no mirror on the right side, gas tank stretched 2 inches. Lenni's pinstripes are a nice touch.

Long and low, Rear fender is Rob Roehl's work, molded, integral taillight is a Donnie Smith trademark.

Side panels fabricated by Rob Roehl are a clever way to introduce something new and still retain the signature shape of the factory covers.

The shocks are from Legends and measure 12 inches in length. Note the three-point mounting of the swingarm pivot, per comments made earlier in the book.

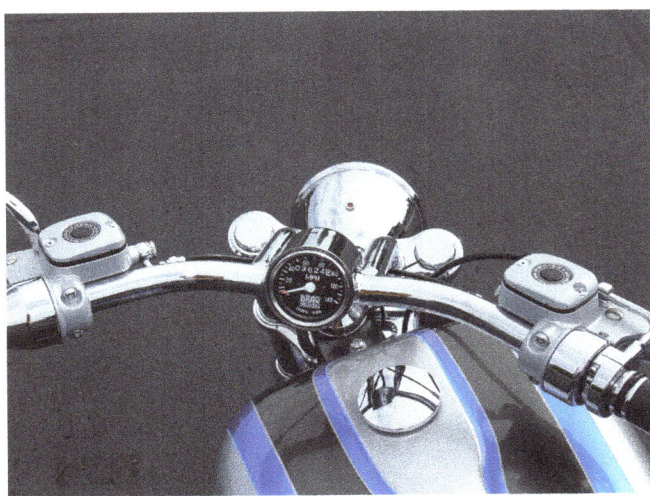

The small speedo in the center of the bars is another Donnie Smith trademark. Hand controls are from Arlen Ness.

Detailed externally, internally the Evo sports a stock bottom end and larger pistons for a displacement of 85 inches. A Crane cam, Keihin carb and SuperTrapp pipe help the Evo run with those Twin Cams.

A stretched tank and a painted panel makes for a great profile.

Builder	Donnie Smith
Year/model	1985 FXR
Engine, year, displacement	H-D 1985, 85 cu. In.
Engine builder	Bill Lackner
Cases	H-D
Cylinders	H-D
Heads	H-D
Aircleaner	H-D
Exhaust	2 into 1, SuperTrapp
Transmission	H-D - 5 Speed, 1994 Road King
Frame, stretch/rake	H-D, 1-1/2 in., 37 deg.
Fork Ass'm	H-D
Triple trees	H-D
Shocks	Legend, 12 inches
Front wheel/tire	H-D, Avon 90/90-19
Rear wheel/tire	H-D 150-16
Calipers	GMA
Sheet metal	H-D
Sheet metal mods	Rob Roehl
Painter	Krazy Kolors, Lenni Schwartz
Paint brand	H of K, Galaxy Grey

panels, he also incorporated a raised section that mimics the shape of the signature FXR side covers used on all the factory bikes. The rear fender is simple to the extreme, complete with the molded-in light assembly and license plate mount – standard Donnie Smith features.

Though the paint was applied by Lenni Schwartz, the design and colors are Donnie's, as he explains: "That paint job is one I've been thinking about for years. The frame is grey, and while the sheet metal is that same grey, there's also some Galaxy Grey from H of K, and a band of process blue. The FXR and Donnie Smith graphics are Lenni's work of course." For wheels, Donnie stayed with the factory cast items, painted to match the rest of the bike, complete with a blue pinstripe, and calipers from GMA painted in the same process blue.

In trying to sum up the latest FXR, Donnie explains that, "the bike really isn't too crazy, but at the same time it's very appealing and gets a lot of attention. The stretched frame and swingarm give it really nice lines, makes it look longer than it really is. And like that first FXR I had, it's always a pleasure to ride."

Factory wheels, nineteen and sixteen inches, are painted to match the rest of the bike.

Chapter Eleven

Neil's Hot Rod FXR

When Neil Ryan decided to build a back-to-basics FXR, he started at the very beginning. "I found a 1982 FXR frame, and title on eBay," explains Neil, "that was the start. At about the same time I bought out a small estate, which included a rather unique engine."

Neil's unique engine is sometimes called a Shovelution, because it's an Evo that's short enough to fit in a Shovel frame. The shorter overall dimensions are achieved by combining a four-inch Sportster flywheel assembly with a set of four-inch bore cylinders for a total of 100 cubic inches.

The bottom end is 100% S&S, as both the cases and the flywheel assemblies are from Viola, Wisconsin. This particular engine was originally built by Lee's Speed Shop for drag racing. Because it was meant to haul ass one quarter mile at a time, Lee used cast iron cylinders from Axtell. Lee chose cast iron because it grows less than aluminum – meaning the hot cylinder is close to the cold dimensions, including the inside of the cylinder, for better ring-seal.

Neil Ryan aboard the hot rod FXR built from an eBay frame and a somewhat unique Evo designed to run the drag strip.

Neil works out of a small garage – which proves all you need is a sturdy hoist, tools and shelves for storage, in order to build custom motorcycles.

Chain drive helps made room for the 150/80-16 tire. Another chain, a conventional-style primary, connects motor and tranny, clutch is late model H-D.

Helping those cylinders inhale and exhale are the heads from STD, aided in their breathing tasks by the Super G carb from S&S and the two-into-one exhaust from Bassani.

When the mock up of the bike started, Neil encountered a series of challenges – because modern parts don't always adapt easily to a frame that's thirty-five years old. Neil chose a 1990 and later inner primary, which meant he could use a later, stronger, five-speed tranny with the splined output shaft, and '98-and-up clutch assembly. In case the later five-speed wasn't quite up to drop-the-hammer hard launches, a trap door and one-piece counter-shaft from Bert Baker were installed for insurance.

Lee's Speed Shot created a 100 cubic inch Evo by combining a 4-inch Sportster flywheel with a 4-inch bore. The combo fits nicely in the factory frame.

Connecting the clutch hub to the compensator sprocket is the standard and durable primary chain we've all seen so many times. A 530 single row chain connects the output shaft to the rear wheel. It was Neil's plan from the start to run a 150/80X16 rear tire. The wheel is a three-inch item from Harley, spoked without any offset. As Neil explains, "I did need some offset to clear the chain however, so I used a spacer on the left to move the wheel to the right, just enough that the two sprockets line up, and the wheel is centered in the frame (from the factory they aren't centered). Then I had to machine .140 inches off the caliper mount on the right side so there was room for everything to fit between the two sides of

Nothing fancy here, just factory-style foot controls and highway pegs, two-into-one exhaust, and an S&S air cleaner bolted to a "G" carburetor.

Front brake uses a four-piston factory caliper and a polished rotor. Fork assembly is a conventional made up of 49mm legs from H-D. Headlight is a H-D item.

the swingarm." The Swingarm itself is 1.750 inches longer than stock, thanks to the crew at Donnie Smith Custom Cycles.

At the other end of Neil's project is another spoked rim, this one wrapped with a 90/90X19 tire. For brakes up front, Neil settled for a single disc and a caliper from Milwaukee. Supporting all that machinery is a 49mm factory wide-glide fork assembly, not only stronger, but lighter than the earlier 35 and 39mm tubes seen on most FXRs. Because the fork assembly was meant to support a 21-inch rim, running the 19-inch up front lowered the nose. All Neil had to do in back was install a set of shorter shocks and bingo, one lowered FXR.

For sheet metal, form follows function. Just a stock rear fender, a nearly stock tank, and a simple aftermarket front fender. Once again, mounting the two fenders and hardware wasn't as simple as it might seem. In the rear, Neil used the stock '82 fender struts and mounted the fender in the factory location. The hard part was mounting the late model turn and marker light, which meant machining both the light assembly and the strut so that when all was done, the light looks like a factory fit on the older strut.

"Up front I had to modify the fender because the wide glide fork was designed for a twenty-one inch wheel," explains Neil, "and I was using a nineteen. That meant the fender wanted to sit up high like a dirt bike. I had to make a new mount on the fender to bring it down low so it hugs the tire. It's one of those little details that make a custom bike custom."

Gas tank is another item from Milwaukee, minus any dash, with Neil's own FXR Racing logo.

The no-BS paint job is more of Neil's back-to-basics approach. The color is a candy red sprayed over a silver base by TJ Design while the tasteful FXR logo was Neil's idea massaged by a friend who just happens to be a graphic artist.

Pointing the way is a set of stock appearing handlebars, supported by four-inch risers. All the switches are '07 and newer, connected to a matching harness hidden inside the bars. The harness runs under the tank where it ties into the early-style FXR harness. Using the later model switches and controls was a lot of work but came with a hidden asset – the ability to use late model turn and marker lights.

The bike was finished and ready just in time for Sturgis (a common phenomenon), which meant Neil had the week to make all the events on the new bike – including the drag races at the Buffalo Chip.

In the end, Neil succeeded with his plan. What started as a bare frame and stand-alone V-twin morphed into a romping FXR that looks good parked with more current and expensive bikes, and just happens to haul ass when the kick stands come up.

Builder	Neil Ryan
Year/model	1982 FXR
Engine, year, displ.	S&S/Axtel, 100 cu. In.
Engine builder	Lee's Speed Shop
Cases	S&S
Cylinders	Axtel
Heads	STD
Aircleaner	S&S
Exhaust	Bassani
Transmission	H-D, 5 Speed, 1994 FXR w Baker trap door
Frame, stretch/rake	H-D, stock
Fork Ass'm	H-D 49mm
Triple trees	H-D
Shocks	Drag Spec. 11-1/2 in.
Front wheel/tire	DNA 19X2.25, Cobra 90/90-19
Rear wheel/tire	H-D 16X3, Cobra 150/80-16
Calipers	H-D
Sheet metal	H-D
Sheet metal mods	Neil Ryan
Painter	TJ Design
Paint brand	H of K

You don't have to do much to an FXR to make one good-looking motorcycle. Neil stayed with the basics; nineteen inch front wheel, sixteen in back, factory tank and rear fender, bright red paint and just enough chrome to make it pop.

Chapter Twelve

Not Another Custom

When Pat Quinn from Massachusetts decided to build one more bike, he decided to build a V-Twin sport bike - not another custom. "My goal was to build a sport bike," explains Pat. "Something fast that would handle great - a demon." To bring the demon to life Pat contacted the Shadley Bros., from Whitman, Massachusetts. Mark Shadley and Pat agreed that the bike would be based on an FXR chassis, and that they would build it as a Café' bike.

After the tear down, there were two piles of parts: keepers, and the swap-meet stuff. The keepers included the frame, some of the sheet metal and hardware. To ensure the demon would indeed be fast, Mark chose an Evo-style crate motor from S&S. Sometimes called the Frankenmotor, Pat's new engine measured 117 cubic inches displacement, a figure achieved by combining a 4.125 inch bore with a 4.375 inch stroke. An S&S Super E carb feeds the beast, while a Bassani exhaust provides an exit for the spent gasses. At a later date, after some break-in miles, the Franken-Beast hit a best of 135 Horses on the Shadley Dyno.

Mark Shadley made only two modifications to the factory frame. To make room for a 150 series rear tire he took the belt-sander to each fender rail, and then reinforced what was left of the rails. The Baker six-speed Mark ordered was the FL model, with the engine's oil tank underneath. Which

As American as apple pie. Born in Milwaukee, built again in Whitman, Massachusetts, powered by 117 cubic inches of V-twin from Viola, Wisconsin.

meant cutting out one crossmember to make clearance for the oil tank, and reinforcing of the frame to compensate for any strength lost to the missing crossmember.

To complete the chassis, Mark installed a Bagger swingarm. "I like to use a 2004-and-up swingarm with the one-inch axle, ¾ inches longer than a stock FXR swingarm," explains Mark. "That pushes the rear wheel back just a little, they're a lot stronger than stock, and they provide plenty of room for a wider wheel and tire." Instead of supporting the swingarm with stock cleve-block rubber bushings, Mark installed a CCE kit with spherical bearings.

While most custom bikes are lowered, Mark chose to raise this one with Ohlins shocks, three-

The Evo design ain't dead yet. Under the DNA air cleaner is an S&S "E" carb feeding two S&S V series heads with valves operated by a .640 cam. Gasses exit with help from a Bassani two-into-one pipe. The net result of all those components working in harmony is 135 horsepower.

With 134 horses turning the rear wheel nothing but chain drive would do. Transmission is a FLH case with the oil tank underneath – thus the missing bulge behind the rear cylinder.

quarters of an inch longer than stock, and front fork tubes a little longer than stock as well. The wheels are Phantom-cut billet wheels from HHI/Renegade Wheels. The four-piston calipers came from the same company, two up front and one in the back.

Pat and Mark decided early on to retain the FXR look. In keeping with that decision the bike carries the near-stock tank, and two fenders with the FXR signature shape though both were fabbed in the Shadley Bros. shop.

The Café' fairing, HID headlight, huge tachometer and bars, are all genuine Milwaukee items. The black pegs, levers and hand controls are RSD

Under the primary cover is a Harley-Davidson primary chain and a lock up Barnett Scorpion clutch. The nicely stitched seat is the work of Corbin.

Taillight is from Joker Machine; license bracket is a Cycle Vision item. Swingarm is from a FLH, stretched ¾ inch. Tall risers carry the Shadley Bros logo, bars and switches are stamped with the bar and shield.

designs. A Joker Machine taillight and Cycle Vision license bracket bring up the rear.

The blue hues were the choice of Pat's ten year old son, while the actual application was a team effort: Ron Abercrombie, a Shadley Brothers' employee, is the man responsible for the Blue Streak and the final, flattening clear; while the silver panels, silver-leaf accents and pinstriping are the work of John Hartnett.

The first road test might be called a trial by fire. Pat shipped the new bike to California and rode it from there to Sturgis. The only trouble he had with the bike had nothing to do with a mechanical breakdowns, and a lot to do with a state trooper in California. Apparently the new FXR is a demon.

Paint is Blue Streak, a Chrysler color. Artwork and silverleaf is the work of John Hartnett. Fairing is a genuine Harley-Davidson item.

Billy from the Shadley crew makes one of many passes for the demanding photographer.

Builder	Shadley Bros.
Year/model	1991 FXR
Engine, year, displ.	S&S 117 cu. In. TC
Engine builder	S&S
Cases	S&S
Cylinders	S&S
Heads	S&S
Aircleaner	S&S
Exhaust	Bassini
Transmission	Baker 6 speed OD
Frame, stretch/rake	H-D, 1991 FXR stock, mod for TC.
Fork Ass'm	H-D tubes, Race Tech spings, valves
Triple trees	H-D
Shocks	Ohlins
Front wheel/tire	Hawg Halters 19X2.1, Mich. 100/90-19
Rear wheel/tire	Hawg Halters 18X4.25, Mich. 150/80-18
Calipers	HHI
Sheet metal	H-D tank, Shadley Bros. fenders
Sheet metal mods	Shadley Bros.
Painter	Shadley Bros.
Paint brand	PPG

Abundant go power requires abundant whoa power – two HHI four-piston calipers up front and one in back, all squeezing rotors from the same manufacturer.

Sitting a bit higher than most customs - this one is designed to haul ass on corners as well as in a straight line. Aiding in the corner department are Ohlin shocks and Harley tubes with Race Tech springs and valving.

Chapter Thirteen

FXR2 by Ness

Given the fact that the later CVO FXRs were produced in limited numbers, it would seem prudent for owners to simply leave their bikes alone. But when the new owner is Arlen Ness, what can you expect?

Way back in the early days when a lot of guys preferred Softails and didn't really dig the FXR at all (too Japanese, too radical a change, didn't look like a chopper at all) Arlen Ness was one of the few to embrace the FXR as both good looking and fast. In other words, a great platform for a custom Harley-Davidson.

Arlen had the eye. And though the early Ness bikes we all remember came with two engines, two blowers and four carburetors, Arlen was very good at creating what might be called mild customs. And the FXRs of the day were a good example. His recipe was simple: take one FXR, drop it, clean up the tank, install some wheels and maybe brakes, hang a café fairing on the front – presto, one very ride-able custom.

The FXR seen here follows that pattern. Note the Ness wheels, 21 inches up front, and 18 in back, complimented by chrome-plated Ness calipers,

The FXR2 started in the hands of Arlen Ness, then moved to Paul Yaffe's shop before passing to the current owner. Thus the bike is a tasteful collaboration of two very talented builders.

No, CVO/FXRs did not come with a Trask air cleaner. Other than that the motor is a stock 80 cubic inch Evo – some would say the best motor they ever made in the best chassis they ever built.

Wheels are Ness designs; note the matching pulley and rotors. Rear wheel is an 18 inch loop with a Avon tire, front is wrapped in another Avon measuring 21 inches in diameter.

the smoothed out tank with missing dash, the mandatory fairing, and the side covers that fill the whole under-seat triangle. Of course there's the taillight license plate mount and (more chrome) fender struts. Add the blue and black paint job by JC Mason and you have one very clean Arlen Ness FXR.

The story doesn't end there however. At some point Arlen sold the bike to a friend we all know, Paul Yaffe. Being a master bike builder, Paul couldn't leave the bike alone either. Thus the more observant readers will see a few items that simply can't be from the mind of Arlen Ness. Like the Monkey bars, the grips, the pegs, and the Trask air cleaner. After personalizing the bike Paul sold it to another friend, a fella by the name of Harlan Schillinger.

Harlan is an avid rider who owns a number of customs. He's also a long time friend of Arlen and Paul's. It's very likely that Paul picked Harlan – as much as Harlan picked the bike – knowing full well that Harlan would be the owner who would simply ride and maintain the bike. Leave it alone in other words as a quiet nod to one exceptional bike builder and designer. As Harlan say's, "I just ride it, in respect to the fine gentleman who made this bike a clean, solid FXR."

Gone are the stock speedo and tach and the dash mounted at the front of the tank. Instead, we have a un-dash, and one large Speedometer.

Monkey bars are another contribution from Paul, license bracket is from Arlen. Shocks are from Legends, seat is a LePera item.

Builder	Ness/Yaffe
Year/model	1999 FXR2
Engine, year, displ.	H-D 80 cu. In. Evo
Engine builder	H-D
Cases	H-D
Cylinders	H-D
Heads	H-D
Aircleaner	Trask
Exhaust	Bassani
Transmission	H-D
Frame, stretch/rake	1999 FXR stock
Fork Ass'm	H-D
Triple trees	H-D
Shocks	Legends
Front wheel/tire	Ness 21, Avon
Rear wheel/tire	Ness 18, Avon
Calipers	Ness
Sheet metal	H-D
Sheet metal mods	
Painter	Ness Inc.
Paint brand	

The man who first put a café fairing on an FXR did it again with this special FXR2. Note the very modern headlight, the Yaffe grips and mirrors, and the factory switches.

Rear rotor matches the 18-inch Ness rim. Caliper is likewise a unique Ness item.

Chapter Fourteen

Timeless Styling

The story of Rodney Robert's FXR is a story of perseverance and what Rodney calls *timeless styling*. The bike started out as a customer build at Rodneys House, in Little Rock, Arkansas. "The customer told me what he wanted," explains Rodney, "basically a hot rod FXR. So we started in with a Kenny Boyce frame and a set of wheels. At the start of the project I gave the guy a list of parts we were going to use and the final price. But, as we went along with the build he requested one change after another. I thought I better give him the new price. Needless to say the project became a pile of parts on the lift in the back of the shop."

"Well, the guys in the shop and I would walk by the hoist and make some comment about what kind of change we could make that would be really cool, but pretty soon someone else had a *better* idea. In the end, we didn't make much progress. In February of 2005 a local promoter came by and asked if we would like to be part of Thunder on the Rock, which featured a build off called, The Great Arkansas Biker Build Off. We were to compete with Jones Harley-Davidson and The Hard Riders. The Build Off was scheduled for June 24 to 26 – in the

A classic custom FXR built on a Kenny Boyce frame in the Rodney's Cycle House shop.

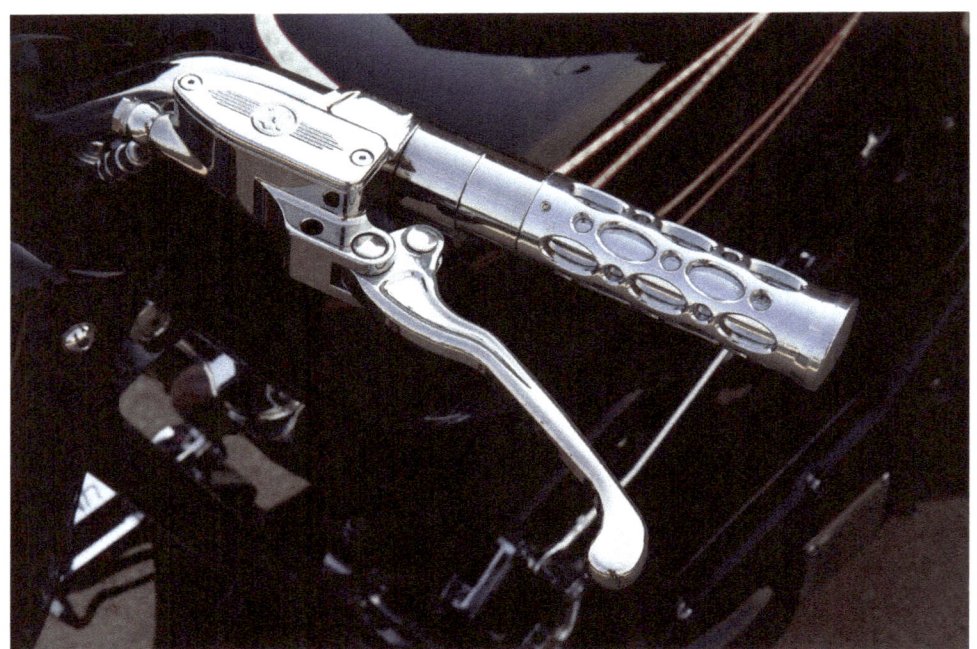

Master cylinders bear the PM logo, ventilated grips are from Ness – first brought to market by Battistinis.

middle of our busy season. I figured the competition were going to build Choppahs, so we decided to take the pile of parts on the lift, and build us a stone cold hot rod."

Rodney already had the Kenny Boyce frame he ordered with a 32-degree neck and enough room at the rear of the frame for a 150 tire and a full-width belt drive. Kenny Boyce frames were notorious for being straight and strong. The only problem was the fact that there weren't many off-the-shelf items that fit Kenny's frame. Thus the oil tank is an early Softail item that required considerable modification and fabrication before it looked like it actually belonged in the frame.

All black with just enough chrome to create a contrast and well-placed scallops, gives this seasoned veteran its timeless appeal.

Gas tank is a Drag Specialties, tweaked to fit the bike and wrap around the seat. Speedo is from VDO, digital tach is from Dakota Digital. Mounting bracket/cover is a fabricated one-off.

Another Evo that will give a Twin Cam a run for its money – 124 cubics and 120 horses. Under the S&S air cleaner is an S&S "G" carb. In fact, other then the two-into-one exhaust this V-Twin is 100% S&S. Note the linkage that stabilizes the transmission-to-motor connection.

The fender struts are straight out of the Ness catalog from the same era as the frame – and like the oil tank – required cutting, welding and machining so they would fit the frame and house two LED lights on each side. For a rear fender, Rodney bought a nine-inch fender from Russ Wernimont (RWS), and then cut off most of the rear half – and trimmed the bottom edge so it would match the line of the fender struts.

For a gas tank, Rodney and crew started with a CCI item designed to fit a Sportster. More fabrication, this time to stretch the tank so it would fit the frame and match the lines of the other components. The front fender is another item from RWS, tweaked just a bit to hug that front tire.

To round out the chassis up front, fork tubes and lower legs from a 1993 FL were combined with triple trees from an early FL. The headlight nacelle that looks so right sitting up front is actually from a 1963 H-D. The front wheel measures nineteen inches in diameter and carries the RC Components logo. Slowing everything down are two, four-piston calipers from PM and rotors that match the wheels. In back, the boys installed a sixteen-inch RC wheel, one PM caliper and one matching rotor. Both of the RC wheels are wrapped in black from Avon, 100/90-19 in front, and 150/80-16 in back.

Rodney is a big believer in that old cliché, that when it comes to cubes, a

The illuminating struts are an Arlen Ness item from back in the day, modernized by Rodney and crew. Fat Avon tire is a 150/80-16, mounted on a RC wheel.

little too much is almost enough. The motor is a 124 S&S Evo, inhaling through a Super G from S&S, and mated to a six-speed transmission from Bert Baker. The mostly black primary houses a conventional chain primary and a Bandit clutch.

Rodney likes his machines simple. That is, all the parts have an essential task. Thus there are no mirrors and only minimal gauges: one speedo from VDO and a small Dakota Digital gauge that's integrated into the fabricated cover for the handle bar clamp. Speaking of handlebars, they came from Drag Specialties, with Ness grips and controls from PM. The forward controls are from UMI Racing, with pegs that match those used on the bars.

Forward controls are UMI item with more Battistini/Ness pegs. Oil tank fits the frame well because it was fabricated for this frame.

When it came time to pick a color, there was only one color in Rodney's palette – black – applied in-house. And lest he be charged with building *another* black Harley, Rodney asked Mike Robbins to break up the black and give the bike a sense of motion, with white goldleaf outlined with red pinstripes.

"When it came time to wire the bike and do the final assembly," recalls Rodney, "I called on an old friend, Eddie Bunch for help. Credit for most of the fabrication goes to Rodney and crew (Jerry for the belt guard and license bracket combo). And for moral support and sandwiches late at night we have Donna to thank."

The story of the too long dormant FXR has a happy ending. Amid a group of fresh choppers, the people at the Build Off knew exactly what they liked the best. Rodney's low-slung FXR won first place hands down.

Not only did the bike take home the trophy, it's a machine that still looks damned good almost fifteen years later – the result of perseverance and timeless styling.

Builder	Rodney's House
Year/model	1994 Special Const.
Engine, year, displ.	124 S&S Evo
Engine builder	S&S
Cases	S&S
Cylinders	S&S
Heads	S&S
Aircleaner	S&S
Exhaust	Two Brothers
Transmission	Biker, 6 Speed
Frame, stretch/rake	Kenny Boyce, 6 deg.
Fork Ass'm	Early H-D w upgrades
Triple trees	H-D
Shocks	Works
Front wheel/tire	RC, Avon 100/90-19
Rear wheel/tire	RC, Avon 150/80-16
Calipers	PM, RC rotors
Sheet metal	Drag Spec. tank, RWD fenders
Sheet metal mods	Rodney's House
Painter	Rodney, Mike Robbions stripes/g-leaf
Paint brand	PPG

Braking is handled by two, PM four-piston calipers up front and one in the rear. Rotors are from RC, designed to match the 16 and 19 inch wheels. The two-into-one pipe is from Two Brothers.

Chapter Fifteen

All about the Motor

Some customs are built around an exceptional paint job, or some sexy fabricated sheet metal. When you look at the FXR built by John Jessup, you realized that in this case it's all about the motor.

First, It's NOT an Evo, or a Shovel for that matter. What it is, is a Twin Cam. Not just any Twin Cam, this one has round cylinders and heads, unusual looking rocker boxes and an air cleaner with two big Rs cut into the face.

Before explaining the motor, it's necessary to explain John's motives in building this FXR. "I built a FXR in 2005." says John. "That was during the recession, my shop was kind of slow and money was tight, so I couldn't buy what I wanted. The bike was assembled with a lot of used parts. At that time I swore the next bike would be built with nothing but the best from the aftermarket."

When John started on bike number two in

Most FXR builders belong to that certain club – HORSEPOWER INC – and John could be the president. Every part of the V-Twin is the best money could buy – carefully assembled by the owner.

Rear view shows off the chain drive to the wheel, which is supported by one of Brock's aluminum swingarms. John's bike sits high – the Super Shox shocks are 12.5 inches long.

John's Twin Cam displaces 124 cubic inches and puts out 155 HP and 160 Lbs. of torque. John achieved that output with help from R&R Cycles, Axtel, H-D and S&S. Compression is 12 to one!

Nineteen RSD front wheel is wrapped with a 100/90-19 inch Michelin tire. To stop the beast John picked Beringer calipers and rotors on both ends.

2015, the economy was better and he definitely kept his promise to himself. The Twin Cam he bought is from 2000, chosen because those early ones will take a 1990 to 1993 primary. Most of the Twin Cam's components went in the spare-parts pile; all of them replaced with carefully chosen high-quality parts.

The bottom end is made up of a Dark Horse flywheel assembly (4-5/8 inch stroke). The pistons carry the CP-Carillo logo, and the tech sheet that came with them said 12 to 1 compression! (4-1/8 inch bore). The stroker crank and large diameter cylinder net out to 124 cubic inches. The aluminum cylinders are from Axtel, topped by billet heads from R&R Cycles. For the cams John picked S&S 640 cams.

Most FXR builders who install a Twin Cam go with a carburetor, to avoid the complexity of EFI. John had other ideas, "I wanted a FXR with fuel injection," explains John. "I work on EFI bikes all the time, I'm very familiar with the systems, so why not." John chose the Power Vision from DynoJet for all of its programing capabilities.

The Twin Cam came with a five-speed gearset, which had to go. Once again John picked the best – a six-speed gearset from Baker, a clutch from Primo/Rivera and a factory, chain-style primary drive. Power to the rear wheel gets there by another chain, this one a single-row number 530.

Setting a Twin Cam in a factory FXR frame isn't rocket science, but there are problems to be resolved – like the clearance problem between the oil pan and the frame's cross braces for example. Rather than cut and move the braces in the 1984 factory frame, John purchased an oil pan from Deviant Fab that allows for clearance between the oil pan and both of the frame braces and the mount for the kickstand.

With the drivetrain set in the freshly painted frame, John turned his energies to everything else; the chassis, the sheet metal and the little things like wiring and controls.

For sheet metal, John decided to use the stock components from a 1989 FXRL. One of the things he didn't reuse was the wiring harness. Rather than use a 30+-year-old bundle of wires, John chose

For sheet metal John stayed with FXR components. Gas tank is from a 1991 Low Rider, modified to accept an electric pump for the EFI.

a new harness for a 2006 Dyna. Because John chose to use EFI on the Twin Cam, he also needed an electric fuel pump in the tank. So before the sanding and painting could start, TPJ Custom installed a Sportster pump inside the tank.

Steve Turnbaugh is responsible for the bright red and the deeper maroon panels, both done with PPG paint; while Adam at Blinkystriping did the pinstripes and the painted factory logo on the sides of the tank. Powder coating from Modesto Plating & Chrome was used for the cylinders.

The nicely detailed cylinders are from Axtel, topped from heads from R&R Cycles. Note the releases – necessary if you want to start a 12 to 1 engine.

The chassis looks like something right out of a display at an industry trade show. The brands read like a who's who in the aftermarket. The billet wheels carry the RSD logo of Roland Sands, while the upside-down fork is from Storz. The brand name Beringer is spelled out across each of the three calipers and on the small fasteners that locate the floating rotors. In back, the beefy aluminum swingarm is from Brock's, supported by two 12.5 inch shocks from Super Shox.

Instead of multiple, round, analog gauges to tell John how much gas is in the tank and whether or not the charging circuit is charging, John decided to rely on the Power Vision EFI controller, already mentioned, that can read any sensor on the bike at the push of a button. The Power Vision also makes it possible to tune the engine on the run, and without a laptop.

The Power Vision is mounted in the center of the bars from Fly Racing and the bars in turn are mounted

EFI controller from Power Vision can display any "gauge" at any time. Bars are from Fly Racing with master cylinders from PM and RSD mirrors.

Builder	John Jessup
Year/model	1984 FXRDG
Engine, year, displ.	124 cu.in. TC
Engine builder	John Jessup
Cases	H-D
Cylinders	Axtel
Heads	R&R Cycles
Aircleaner	R&R Cycles
Exhaust	Tom White Racing
Transmission	2000 Baker 6 Speed
Frame, stretch/rake	H-D stock
Fork Ass'm	Storz/Ceriani inverted
Triple trees	
Shocks	Super Shox 12.5 in.
Front wheel/tire	RSD 19, Michelin
Rear wheel/tire	RSD 18, Michelin
Calipers	Beringer
Sheet metal	H-D
Sheet metal mods	TPJ Custom EFI tank mod
Painter	Steve Turnbaugh, Adam @ Blinky striping
Paint brand	

to the two 11" risers made by Hardcase Performance. The grips and controls are from Performance Machine while the foot pegs are genuine Harley items.

"When we finally finished the bike in 2017," explains John, "I spent some time with it on the Dyno. After the dial-in and some break in miles were finished, we did the final tweaks and the dyno runs. The 124 Twin Cam put out 155 horses and 160 foot pounds of torque at 7000 RPM. The next stop was the FXRs of California Bike Show, sponsored by Hot Bike, where we won Best of Show. Since then, the bike has garnered 6 more Best of Show trophys."

"Now, I feel like the show part of the deal is done," explains John. "I've been using and abusing it more and more, and I have to say, it's a gas to ride. I always tell people, 'I'm not a bike builder, I'm a mechanic and a shop owner.' The bike turned out so good, I've surpassed my goals."

The small Café fairing is just big enough to knock a whole in the wind and take some pressure off the rider.

The FXR frame is totally stock, front wheel from RSD measures nineteen inches wrapped by Michelin rubber.

Chapter Sixteen

Lean and Mean

The FXR of Tom Edison defies easy definition. It has an RT fairing, but it doesn't have the bags or a tour-pak - two items that make an RT an RT. And it ain't no drag race queen with the extra wide rear tire and NOS bottle. A restoration it isn't either, way too many aftermarket and one-off components for that.

Considering the fact that the owner, Tom Edison, is a life-long drag racer, maybe this bike is one person's version of a high performance road rocket. "I've done a lot of racing," says Tom, "and I've always liked bikes that are lean and mean."

Like a lot of customized Harleys, this one has lived a number of lives. "I've owned the bike for 27 years," says Tom. "At one point I ran a 124 inch engine, and I thrashed it again and again, on the track and on the highway, until finally I blew that motor to smithereens."

After the catastrophic death of that oversize Evo, Tom's FXR went into a long sleep in the back corner of the shop. As Tom explains it, "I had other bikes to ride in the meantime, until finally in the spring of 2019 I decided to put it all back together."

When Tom cleaned out the shop, low and behold, he found a frame, the makings of an Evo, 2 wheels, a 5-speed transmission and numerous smaller items, i.e. enough to make a nice FXR with an RT fairing.

Tom's RT rolls on RC wheels – a 19 inch up front and a 16 in back, both wear Shinko tires, 100/90-19 and 150-16 on front and back. Fairing is a JD Fabrications creation.

With a long history of drag racing, Tom picked components that work – mid-controls and simple highway pegs. Under the primary cover is a H-D chain connected to a Barnett clutch assembly.

An inventory showed a mostly complete FXR, minus the motor of course. In addition, Tom had a considerable stash of high performance components stashed here and there.

"Sturgis 2019 became my goal."

Like most builders, Tom started with the frame – that went to the powder coat shop for a fresh coat of bulletproof gloss black. For a swingarm Tom decided to use a Trac Dynamics aluminum arm - four inches longer that stock – that he already had in-stock so to speak.

The swingarm wasn't the only thing Tom had left over from past drag

Front fender is a swap meet special. Lighting the way when the sun goes down is a Daymaker headlight.

bikes and assorted projects. "Bill Gardner (owner of GMA) was a friend of mine prior to his passing," explains Tom. "At one point he designed a rear-wheel caliper with an integral bracket, and I just happen to have one. It wasn't meant for a FXR, but that didn't mean I couldn't make it work."

For wheels, Tom chose aluminum wheels from RC Components, "I really like those older RC Components wheels, and I had both a 16X4.5 inch rear wheel and a front wheel that measured 19X3 inches."

The mid-glide Ceriani fork assembly started life on a Kenny Boyce chassis, and Tom picked it up from a friend, complete with the triple trees. The Brembo four-piston caliper was another "found in the back of the shop" item, bolted to the left side fork leg with a fabricated mounting bracket. The rotors, front and rear, are from Hog Pro, both were pulled out of the metal recycle container when Hog Pro downsized and a bunch of NOS and discontinued parts had to go.

When it came time to find a V-Twin, Tom started with a clean sheet of paper. "I had a set of stock Harley cases, and also a set of Nickosil cylinders from Revolution Industries. For pistons I bought a pair or Wiseco, 10.5 to 1 forged pistons. I had a set of Harley heads in good condition. I took all those pieces and dropped them off at Paul's Cycles in Canogo Park, California.

For a camshaft Tom picked an EV 27 from Andrews, a cam that's been around for a long time. "For any Evo under about 90 inches," says Tom, "that cam is hard to beat, it really pulls from off-idle to red line." The carb is a Miikuni 42, and for an exhaust Tom shortened a Hooker two-into-one system. The combination of slightly oversize cylinders and a stock bottom end netted Tom an 85 inch hot rod Evo.

For a transmission, Tom used a close-ratio five-speed with back-cut gears, built by Sharpeye Ent., in a Delkron case. A Barnett Scorpion clutch with billet basket ensures that when Tom drops the hammer the only thing slipping is the rear tire.

Joker Machine mirrors mount in the ends of Mal Ross Customs bars. Switches are H-D as is the master cylinder. Speedo (0 to 160) carries the Autometer logo.

The rear fender is a RSD item, held in place by two one-off struts. 11.5 inch Works Performance shocks support the Track Dynamic aluminum swingarm.

Part of what gives this FXR it's unique look is Tom's choice of "sheet metal." What catches your eye when you first see the bike is the classic FXRT fairing. When the RT came out no one liked the fairings, "too Japanese" the old-timers said. Eric Buell had a hand in the design of the Japanese fairing. Anyone who's ridden behind one of these will appreciate Eric's skills and the way the fairing punches a hole in the air - an especially nice feature in the rain. Today there's enough demand for that old Japanese fairing to support a healthy aftermarket – Tom bought this example from Jerry at JD Customs.

Just behind the fairing is a factory FXR gas tank, topped by a non-factory carbon fiber dash of unknown origin that was gleaned from a friend in the parts trade. The front fender is a swap-meet special, and the rear is from Russ Wernimont, shorter and fatter - at 7.5 inches wide – than the stock offerings. Struts supporting the fender are a design by Bill Gardner of GMA fame.

The license plate hangs vertically on the left side in a bracket from Hi Tech that includes the LED taillight. Definitely not from the factory are the side covers; the vented design is the work of Outlaw Customs.

The other thing that sets Tom's ride aside from all the others is the paint job. At first it looks like the bike is unfinished, just slapped together from whatever he had in the shop. In reality, he actually planned this black and red paint job, and after the initial shock, it works.

Supporting the front end is a seldom seen Cerianni fork. Front brake is a four-piston Brembo caliper and a Hog Pro rotor.

As Tom explains, "years ago I mocked up a bike in my shop, and all I had was two black fenders and a burnt-orange gas tank. And I'll be damned if it didn't look good sitting on the hoist. So, when I started working on this bike, I had Jake at the Accurate Collision Center in Rancho Cordova, CA paint the tank and side covers with PPG 'Caught Red Handed' a Cadillac color. With the exception of the dash, all the other body parts are painted gloss black."

With any good build, the details are just as important as the size of the motor. Gauges include a gas gauge from Milwaukee and a ProCycle electric speedo from Autometer. Handlebars are H-D Sportster with knurled grips from Mal Ross World Class Custom and Joker Machine bar-end mirrors.

Switches and housings are OEM H-D. Shining the way at night is a DayMaker LED headlight. For comfort, Tom chose a solo seat from Corbin.

Sturgis was the deadline for the new bike, and Tom was there with the FXR he rode from the LA area. The new machine worked so well he took the long way home – via Washington State - making it a 4000+-mile trip.

Builder	Tom Edison
Year/model	1988 FXR-SP
Engine, year, displ.	H-D 1993, 85 cu.in. Evo
Engine builder	Paul's Cycles
Cases	H-D
Cylinders	Revolution Ind, Nikosil
Heads	H-D
Aircleaner	Mikuni
Exhaust	Hooker, modified
Transmission	Delkron, 5 Speed
Frame, stretch/rake	1988 stock
Fork Ass'm	Storz/Ceriani
Triple trees	
Shocks	Works, 11.25 in.
Front wheel/tire	RC 19X3, Shinko 100/90-19
Rear wheel/tire	RC 16X4.5, Shinko 150 - 16
Calipers	Brembo front, GMA rear
Sheet metal	H-D tank, rear fender RWD, front swap mt.
Sheet metal mods	Tom Edison windshield
Painter	Jake @ Accurate Collision
Paint brand	PPG

The Carbon Fiber dash is mounted on a stock FXR gas tank. Solo seat is from Corbin.

Chapter Seventeen

Road Runner

Lars Rydstrom and the Shadley brothers have been friends for several years; each summer they join a group of guys who ride from California to Sturgis. During one of those rides Lars shared with Mark his idea for a custom 'RT – something sexy, but also a bike he could run hard across country. For his part, Mark already had already an idea of a FXRT with a fuel-injected Twin Cam for power.

By the time Lars left Sturgis that year he and Mark had already agreed on a custom FXRT, one that could eat up the miles the way a German Shepherd eats up left overs from the local steak house. The details, however, were worked out during another ride on another continent. That ride took a small group, including Mark, brother Paul, and Lars, through the backcountry of Southern France. The ride gave builder and customer a chance to work together to sort out most of the smaller issues concerning the build. In the end, Lars gave Mark a green light for any additional creative decisions that came up during the building process.

Not too long after the Shadleys landed back in the US of A, a clean and complete FXRT appeared at the Shadley Bros. shop, via Lars and Ebay.

Lars, owner of this FXRT, wanted something that could cover some ground – a cross-country machine – and that's exactly what he got.

After stripping the factory RT down to a frame, and modifying that frame, it was time to start the mock-up.

Mark decided to use a Switchback tank, as it already has an EFT fuel pump installed – but the tank still had to modified to fit over an enlarged top tube.

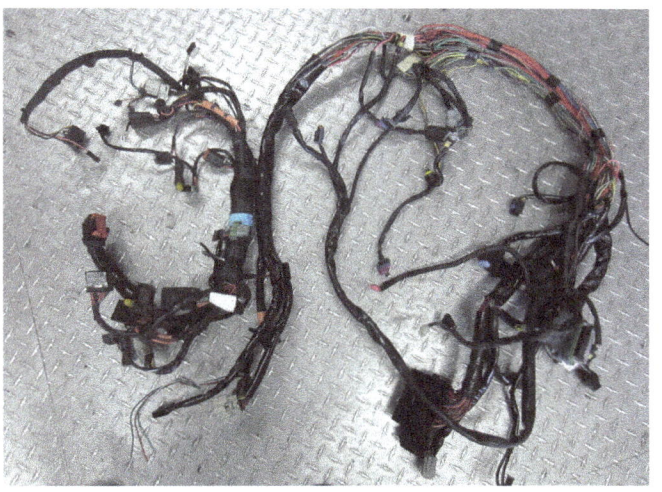

The plan for the bike included a Twin Cam with EFI, which created the need for a fat late model fuel injection harness.

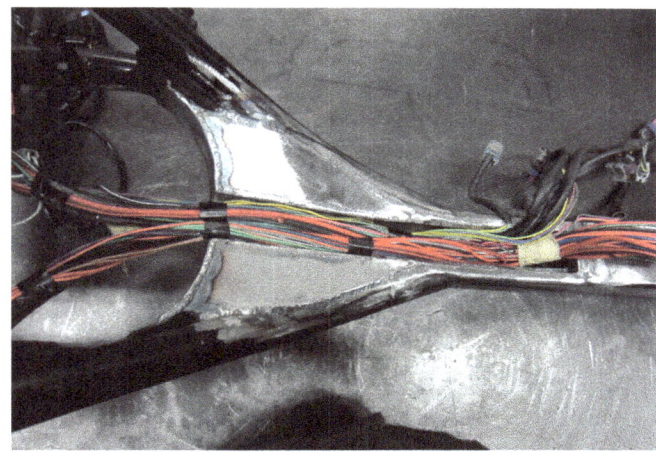

You can see just how fat the harness became, mostly due to the EFI, and why the top tube had to be enlarged to make room for all those wires.

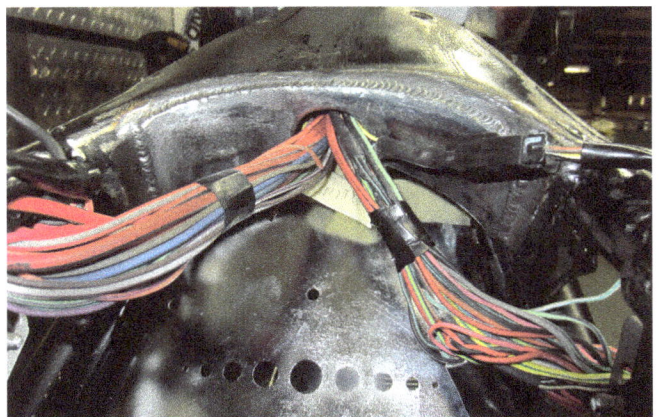

The harness comes out under the seat, and splits into two smaller bundles.

Much farther along, it's starting to look like a motorcycle with a finished wiring harness and a Twin Cam that's almost ready to run. Swingarm is a stretched late model FLH item.

83

The Twin Cam dates to 2007. Originally a 96 inch stocker, a set of Screamin' Eagle big-bore cylinders and pistons bumped the displacement to 113.

As often happens with a build like this, once the old girl was stripped down to the bare frame there weren't a whole lot of usable parts left over, except the frame itself and most of the fairing and bag components.

As mentioned elsewhere in this book, dropping a Twin Cam into a factory frame requires some fairly major modifications to the frame – like moving both braces that run across the bottom of the frame to make room for the Twin Cam oil pan.

Additional modifications to the frame included modifications to the backbone to make room for a late model fuel injection wiring harness. Mark cut out the lower half of the backbone and fabbed up a new lower half that made room for the harness and also made it essentially invisible.

Fuel injection necessitated an electric fuel pump and rather than modify a FXR tank, Mark simply started with a DYNA Switchback tank, one with the pump already installed. Of course the tank wouldn't drop down over the backbone, which required modifying the tunnel. Before the new tank could be set down on the backbone for good, Mark and crew

The rear three-quarter view shows off the sleek lines of this highway hauler. Wheels are from Roland Sands, front carries a 110/90-19, rear is wrapped in a 160/60-18, both from Metzler.

had to make further sheet metal modifications to both the front and tail end of the tank, until it truly looked like it belonged on the RT.

For a Twin Cam motor, Mark started with a stock 2007 model, punched out to 113 cubic inches with a Screamin' Eagle big bore-kit. Additional Screamin' Eagle parts include high-lift cams and a 58mm billet throttle body. Mated to the Twin Cam is a six-speed transmission with SAA gears. Connecting the engine and six-speed is a stock primary chain, and a fresh clutch assembly complete with a heavy duty Screamin' Eagle spring. To tell the injectors when and how much to squirt, Mark picked an EFI controller from Thunder Max.

Though the original fairing was complete, it was also in need of some serious help. For added strength the Dakota Digital gauges, indicator lights and stereo components were mounted and secured with a metal face and backing plates rather than fiberglass and plastic. The fairing itself was also structurally stiffened, remolded and reinforced to ensure it was road worthy after some 30 years of abuse.

Rather than use the stock 35mm tubes, a later 39mm assembly from Milwaukee mounted in the neck – which was left in the same position as when the frame was manufactured in 1985. Holding up the other end of the bike are a pair of Progressive Suspension shocks. The lower end of those shocks bolts to a swingarm borrowed from a 2007 FLHT, which means

Rear fender is from RWD, modified by the Shadley Bros. License bracket and light are Cycle Vision items. Hiding under the clam-shell bags are a pair of Progressive shocks.

The bright yellow and black paint job is the work of the John Hartnett, using PPG urethanes.

A clean and nicely detailed motor – all black with just enough polished fins to make it stand out.

the 'arm is about two inches longer than the original FXR swingin' arm.

To make room for a 160/60-18 rear wheel Mark removed material from the inside of the rear frame section, then reinforced the frame members to compensate for the missing material. Instead of using a chain to help make room for the 160 Metzler tire, Mark and crew used a narrow belt.

PM provided the four-piston caliper used in back, matched to a Roland Sands rotor and pulley. Likewise the brakes up front; except that there are two PM calipers and matching rotors not just one. And like the rear, the front wheel is from PM and measures 19 inches in diameter and carries a 110/90-19 Metzler tire.

Bars from Flanders mounted on Bitwell risers and switches from Milwaukee. Gauges carry the Dakota Digital name, mirrors from Arlen, and the fabricated dash compliments of Mark Shadley.

Finishing up the smaller components is a Mark Shadley dash with Dakota Digital gauges. Pointing the way are Flander's bars mounted in Bitwell risers with mirrors from Arlen Ness so Lars could easily see the blinking red lights coming-up behind.

The license mount is from Randy Aaron at Cycle Vision, the same company that supplied the taillight and blinkers. Seat is branded with the Corbin logo, while the stereo is from Jenson wired to a pair of Focal speakers. The black and yellow paint is a team effort by the crew at the Shadley's shop and local phenomenon John Hartnett.

The yellow with black stripes gives the bike a sense of motion while standing still. But this one is no showboat. With roughly 125 horses, Lars' bright RT will suck the white stripes right off the asphalt as it roars by.

Builder	Shadley Bros.
Year/model	1985 FXRT
Engine, year, displ.	H-D 113 cu. In. TC
Engine builder	Mark Shadley
Cases	H-D
Cylinders	Screamin' Eagle
Heads	H-D Screamin' Eagle
Aircleaner	PM
Exhaust	Vance & Hines
Transmission	H-D 2007 FLHT
Frame, stretch/rake	FXRT, stock
Fork Ass'm	H-D 39mm
Triple trees	H-D
Shocks	Progressive
Front wheel/tire	RSD 19X2.15, Metzler 110/90-19
Rear wheel/tire	RSD 18X4.125, Metzler 160/60-18
Calipers	PM
Sheet metal	Tank H-D 2014 Dyna, fenders RWD mod.
Sheet metal mods	Shadley Bros.
Painter	John Hartnet
Paint brand	PPG

Brother Paul takes the FXRT for a road test.

Chapter Eighteen

Arlen & Arlin

This particular FXR could be said to be the result of work by the Arlen and Arlin team. The genesis of this FXR started late in the 1990s, when Arlin Fatland, owner of 2Wheelers In Denver, Colorado, decided to build something different for a customer. A longtime friend of Arlen Ness, Arlin turned to the Ness catalog for the major components.

The components Arlin purchased from Arlen were somewhat unique, available only from Arlen. As a result the machine took on a look all its own. In fact, looking at the bike now, most riders would never categorize this bike as an FXR. But FXR it is, in the sense that it's built around the basic geometry, and the three-flexible-drivetrain mounts, designed by Harley-Davidson.

"Some of us had already used what Arlen called 'tail dragger' fenders on projects of our own, mostly on the back of our choppers" recalls Arlin. "So I decided to use two of those fenders, a nicely shaped gas tank, and one of Arlen's stretched FXR chassis, as the starting point."

By that time, Arlen had a complete catalog, with enough parts to build pretty much a complete

Arlen Ness kept adding more and more components to his catalog, and eventually had nearly all the components needed to make a complete motorcycle.

Plenty of signature Arlen Ness here; Taildragger fenders, the rear example supported by those unique struts. Holding it all together is one of Arlen's stretched FXR frames.

motorcycle. Thus the V-twin and five-speed tranny, along with the primary components, all came from the Arlen Ness catalog. The motor displaced 88 cubic inches, and came to the 2Wheeler shop completely polished and sporting all the then-current Ness branded covers including the outer primary and derby cover, the cam cover on the right side and of course the rocker boxes. The five-speed transmission came in the same condition, with a polished case and Ness covers.

Eighteen inch spoked rims, also from Arlen, grace both ends of the bike.

In front, the tire is a 140/70-18 Metzler, and in back the numbers on the sidewall read: 200/65-18.

No Ness frame would be complete without Arlen's two-rail swingarm. Note the wrap-around cover for the oil tank and electronics.

Builder	Arlin Fatland
Year/model	2002 Ness Spec. Construction
Engine, year, displ.	2002, 88 cu. In.
Engine builder	Ness
Cases	S&S
Cylinders	S&S
Heads	S&S
Aircleaner	S&S
Exhaust	Ness
Transmission	Ness, 5 Speed
Frame, stretch/rake	Ness, Luxury Liner, 5 in. 35 deg.
Fork Ass'm	Ness, Wide Glide
Triple trees	Ness
Shocks	Progressive
Front wheel/tire	Ness, Metzler 140/70-18
Rear wheel/tire	Ness, Metzler 180/60-18
Calipers	Ness
Sheet metal	Ness
Sheet metal mods	
Painter	Stan Swank
Paint brand	H of K

For brakes, Arlin and crew used a single, Ness four-piston caliper and matching rotor on the front wheel. The rear brake assembly is essentially the same as the front; one four-piston caliper and one polished rotor.

A simple machine, Arlin's creation sports no speedo or tachometer. There is a headlight of course – from the Ness catalog – the same source used for the frenched-in license mount and taillight. Pointing the way is a Ness handlebar with integral risers. Both the hydraulic clutch and the front brake use chrome master cylinders, the grips use the same carved-from-billet design seen throughout the engine and transmission covers.

In keeping with the rest of the bike, Arlin chose a somewhat under stated paint job. The process blue with ghost flames is the work of a local Denver painter, Stan Swank, now residing in the paint booth high in the sky.

Today, this rather unique Arlin and Arlen design is the property of Ian Chastanger, another son of Chaz. Over the years, the original owner sold the bike back to 2Wheelers, and Arlin would sometimes loan the blue FXR to Ian for local Denver rides. Ian liked it so much it just seemed easier to buy it, and not be all the time borrowing the machine.

So, the aging fruit of two bike builders is still alive and well. Owned, ridden and cared for by a rather young rider, roughly the same age as Arlin and Arlen when this tail dragger was created.

Chrome and polish wherever you look. Engine and tranny covers are another series of matching Arlen Ness components.

Chapter Nineteen

Did it Myself

Die hard, long-term riders all share a serious concern. No, it's not which bike to buy next, or what color to paint that project bike in the garage. No, the issue we all share is the lack of young men and women riding on two wheels.

So, it's nice to know that there are some riders from the younger generations stepping into that void, and that not only do they ride, some also build and rebuild their own bikes. Nick Chastagner is one of those individuals. He started building his own bike, the very clean FXRT seen here, well before he graduated from high school.

It all started when Nick was a junior in high school. He had a deal with his father, known to friends as Chaz. Chaz said that he would give Nick a project bike, but Nick had to have it running by the time he graduated from high school.

Thus started Chaz' search for just the right bike. After phone calls to friends and fellow riders, Chaz heard about a pretty complete FXRT in Minnesota. Kurt Peterson, owner of Lil' Evil shop in Perham, MN, said the RT in question was all there, though it needed some love. When Chaz pulled up to the shop and inspected the bike, he found that yes, it was mostly all there, and that yes, it certainly did need love.

What was a rolling wreck is now a classic motorcycle, better looking and faster, than when it came off the line in 1985.

Nick, owner and builder learns first hand how much fun it really is to build and rebuild an old motorcycle.

Starting the reassembly. One powder coated stock frame, stock tubes and wheels.

When it came to the engine Nick hauled the motor to Mike Savage's shop for a thorough overhaul.

Looks like chaos, but it's actually progress. Though there are numerous hoists on the market, if you look over most of the hoists in professional shops they're from Handy Industries.

The annual March Donnie Smith show sent Nick home with his first trophy.

Getting' there. The original wiring harness was put back into service after an inspection and some careful repair.

Mike Savage installed new bearings in the bottom end, bored the cylinders, installed 10.5 to 1 pistons, gave the heads a 5-angle valve job and installed an Andrews EV 27 cam.

"We put the RT in the back of my pickup and drove home to Colorado," recalls Chaz. "When I got home I just left the bike in the truck and parked the truck in the garage. The following day was Nick's birthday, so I made it Nick's birthday present, and reminded Nick that our original deal was still in force – the bike had to be a finished runner by the time he graduated. This was in November of Nick's junior year of high school."

Nick started in on his new project by tearing the bike down to the bare frame. Once the bike was diminished to a big pile of fenders, wheels, and drivetrain components, the parts were sorted into logical groups. Next came the to-do list: What was missing, which parts needed paint, which should go to outside shops and which could be used as-if after only a good inspection and cleaning.

Nick decided the frame and swingarm should be powder coated, instead of painted. Some builders stretch the swingarm or use a slightly longer arm. Nick left his with the stock dimensions, though he had it reinforced before dropping it off with the frame at Prestige Powder Coat in Denver.

Parts to be painted were dropped off at Motor-Sport Concepts in Denver. Given the fact that the bike was over 30 years old, the various steel and 'glass parts required some of that "love" that Kurt warned Chaz about when he picked up the bike. But with a little filler and a lot of sanding, the parts were brought back to their original dimensions, minus all those small dings and dents. The color Nick chose is black cherry, a two-stage Harley-Davidson hue, requiring only the color itself, followed by a few clearcoats and a thorough buffing when all was said and dry.

While the body parts were getting sanded, painted and sanded again, Nick

Most of Nick's FXRT is original – calipers, front fender, fairing, and bags.

The single-piston calipers are the original H-D units, matched up in this case with floating rotors, not stock but also from H-D.

dropped the stock Evo at the shop of Mike Savage in Denver. Long time Harley mechanic and shop owner, Mike gave Nick's V-Twin a thorough going through. That included a complete disassembly and new bearings and seals for the bottom end. "We did bore the cylinders ten-over," says Mike, "and installed new pistons with 10.5 to 1 compression. We also did a five-angle valve job, and installed an Andrews EV 27 camshaft. The carb that we used is a S&S Super E, we ordered the carb and the manifold from S&S." For ignition, the choice was a Dyna system, an ignition that Mike calls, "absolutely bullet-proof." For exhaust Nick picked a two-into-one from Bassani, which had to be modified by Randy Hocker to fit and flow better with the FXRT clamshell bags.

Rather than simply rebuild the original FXR five speed transmission with the tapered output shaft, Nick used the gearset from a 1999 FLT transmission. In addition to the strength benefits of the splined mainshaft, the more modern gearset meant modern clutch assemblies could be used as well – like a nice heavy duty clutch from Barnett connected to

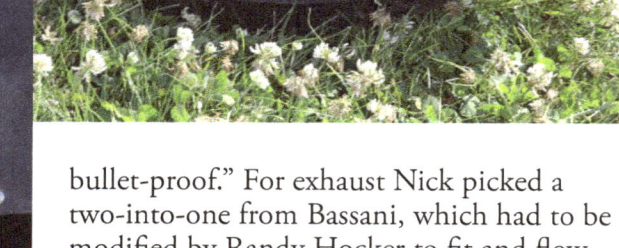

Handlebars are from Drag Specialties, with the club-style riser. Switches are from Harley-Davidson along with housings. Gauges and mount are more original H-D components.

the V-twin by the tried and true primary chain from Milwaukee.

When it came time to assemble the bike, Nick started with the chassis of course. Up front the skinny 35mm fork assembly was left in the corner of the garage, replaced with a 39mm assembly from a Dyna, with springs from Progressive, mated to Dyna triple trees. Stopping is left to two, single-piston H-D calipers matched up with floating aftermarket rotors.

Like the front end of the chassis, the rear end was assembled with a few upgrades. Like the reinforced swingarm, and the use of spherical bearings instead of the stock cleve blocks used by the factory. The shocks Nick picked are 14.5 inch Progressive 490 models. For a rear caliper, Nick picked another factory caliper and the stock rotor. Final touches include a Lepara seat, an 8-inch riser and club-style bars with Harley controls.

When the final assembly was all finished up, Nick not only met the deadline – he was at least three months early. The first long trip the "new" RT took was in a trailer from Denver to St. Paul. Readers might scowl at the mention of a trailer, but trailers are necessary if you're bringing a motorcycle from Denver to St. Paul, MN to attend the Donnie Smith Show (in March). At the show, Nick got plenty of attaboys from the fans and a trophy from the judges.

Roughly five months later Nick proved that the RT was more than a trailer queen – by riding from California to Sturgis, without any problems along the way. While in Sturgis, Nick showed the FXRT at the FXR Show and took 3rd place.

All of which just goes to show that there's hope for those youngsters, and that a little encouragement from the rest of us never hurt a bit.

Builder	Nick Chastagner
Year/model	1985 FXRT
Engine, year, displ.	H-D 1985, 83 cu. In. Evo
Engine builder	Mike Savage
Cases	H-D
Cylinders	H-D
Heads	H-D
Aircleaner	Ness
Exhaust	Trask
Transmission	H-D 5 Speed
Frame, stretch/rake	Stock
Fork Ass'm	H-D
Triple trees	H-D
Shocks	Progressive, 14.5 in.
Front wheel/tire	H-D, Metzler 100/90-19
Rear wheel/tire	H-D, Metzler 130-19
Calipers	HD
Sheet metal	H-D Stock
Sheet metal mods	
Painter	Motorsports Concepts
Paint brand	

Under the primary cover is a typical Harley primary chain, and a later model Barnett clutch assembly made possible by the more modern main shaft.

Chapter Twenty
Top Shelf

Some people drink whatever the bar is serving. Cheap-ass whiskey that burns like kerosene is good enough – who cares. And then there are those who insist that the bartender reach to the top shelf for the expensive Scotch or that certain smooth and hard-to-find Tequila.

When Bob Zeolla decided to build a very specific custom FXR, he made the bartender – Dave Perewitz in this case – reach all the way to the top shelf and then some.

"I wanted a FXR, and it had to be a Shovel," explains Bob. "I've owned a lot of Shovels, so I decided if I was going to buy a FXR, it had to be a Shovel. The build took three years, partly because I changed what I wanted during the building process, and partly because everything had to be the best."

Dave Perewitz explains that the FXR Bob bought was already customized, complete with a raked neck. And Bob wanted stock dimensions. "So after stripping the bike down, one of the first things we had to do was cut off the neck and weld it back on, with the same rake – 30 degrees - the bike

One very cool old FXR modernized to the max with cutting edge components more often seen on sport bikes.

The belt primary is from BDL. Note the coils – sparking two plugs per cylinder.

Bob's Shovel is a stock 1982 model, mostly stock inside, but dressed up outside with careful assembly and Sera Coating of the rocker boxes and most of the covers.

had when it was new. The next big snag came when Bob decided he wanted a 170-rear tire. Even with a chain drive, there isn't enough room for that fat tire in a FXR frame. We had to cut off the back of the frame, widen it and weld it all together again, that was a lot of work."

Widening the back of the frame was only part of the modifications necessary to make it possible to ride away with a fat tire FXR.

As David explains, "The bike came with the early tranny with the tapered shaft. We had to start by switching the guts of the transmission to a more modern five-speed gearset. I was able to get an extended main shaft from PM, but then we still had to move the primary over with a spacer and offset pulley from BDL, the manufacturer of the primary belt drive. Of course the stock factory swingarm wouldn't work either, so we called Brock's Performance for one of their very light and strong aluminum swingarms."

The necessary cutting, welding and transmission modifications didn't happen all at once. "It was like two steps forward and three back," recalls Bob. "Sometimes the bike sat on the hoist for quite a long time… waiting for parts or for me to make a decision."

For chassis parts Bob told the bartender to reach for that expensive Tequila again. Up front he picked an upside-down fork assembly from Ohlins. On the other end, Bob chose 13-inch piggyback shocks from that same company. The brakes too came off the upper shelves - the six-piston calipers carry the Beringer logo and squeeze Lyndall rotors.

Just because Bob wanted 'Busa suspension and sport bike rubber for an old Harley, didn't mean he wanted to give up the FXR identity. The tank is stock, the real deal from Milwaukee, complete with gauges in their stock location. Not so stock are the often seen triangular side covers from the Arlen Ness catalog.

Fenders are from Russ Wernimont (RWD). The rear fender, though not a Harley item, was an easy item to mount. "But the front fender, that was workout," says David. "They don't make wrap-around fenders that work with the upside-down forks. Mounting the front fender would seem to be a simple project, but it was a lot of work to design and then fabricate those brackets."

Breathing starts with an S&S Super E carb and ends with two-into-one pipe. Note, the mid-controls with dirt bike pegs.

The upside-down fork is from Ohlin, supporting a 19-inch rim from Lyndall – the same company that made the rotors. Calipers are six-piston beauties from Beringer.

After reaching to the top for chassis and sheet metal choices, Bob did a turn around concerning the motor when he told David to leave it stock. "We gave the Shovel a face lift," says David. "We pulled the top end apart and it looked good, and the motor already had a mild cam from Andrews, so we just detailed the motor as we reassembled it with new gaskets. While it was apart, we sent most of the engine and transmission covers to Krazy Kustoms and had them Sera Coat the parts. I liked the coating because it's very durable, and the color we chose works well with the bronze color used on some of the Ohlins components."

Two of the last components to be purchased were the wheels. "I wasn't sure what to buy," explains Bob, "it was Jody Perewitz who found the wheels. They're Lyndall wheels from Western Power Sports, and they're just perfect for the bike."

For handlebars Bob requested a set of low-rise black bars from Hardcase Performance mounted to the top tree with MJK risers. The master cylinders - the clutch is hydraulic - and mirrors are from PM and finished in black to match everything else on the bars. For foot controls Bob chose components with a certain dirt-bike look from MJK.

Don't look for blinkers, or for wiring. If there were two things Bob was certain of from the very beginning it was the turn signals and the harness.
As Bob puts it, "I didn't want anything that wasn't necessary. No signals, I didn't even want a horn. And David and I agreed that all the wires would be run out of sight."

The Blue with the sparkle is a 2017 Ford

The yellow, orange, red flames are the work of the master – David Perewitz – outlined by another pro, Keith Hanson.

Builder	Perewitz
Year/model	1982 FXR
Engine, year, displ.	H-D 1982, 74 cu. In. Shovel
Engine builder	Perewitz
Cases	H-D
Cylinders	H-D
Heads	H-D
Aircleaner	
Exhaust	Stainless, Perewitz
Transmission	1991 H-D, w extended main shaft
Frame, stretch/rake	H-D Stock
Fork Ass'm	Ohlins, inverted
Triple trees	Brock's
Shocks	Ohlins, 13 in.
Front wheel/tire	Lyndall, Avon 100/90-19
Rear wheel/tire	Lyndall, Avon 170/60-17
Calipers	Beringer
Sheet metal	Tank H-D, fenders RWD
Sheet metal mods	Perewitz
Painter	Perewitz, pinstripes Keith Hanson
Paint brand	PPG

color: Kona Blue from PPG. Bob saw the color on a Mustang near the end of the project and told David he could do what he wanted with the flames, but he had to use the Kona Blue for the dominant color.

The overlapping yellow-orange-red flames are pure Perewitz and explain in a glance why David is called the king of flames. Perhaps the only thing better than a set of Perewitz flames, is a set that are pinstriped by Keith Hanson – a combination of traditional lighter blue outlines and a second set of stripes done with goldleaf.

It took a long time, and many late nights drinking that expensive Tequila. But in the end it was all worthwhile. Because unlike liquor, building a custom motorcycle is a party that only a few can attend. And unlike the party at the bar, the party at the shop gets better and better and doesn't really hit the high point until the project is done – and the rider can put a leg over the seat, fire it up and experience a high better even than Tequila can deliver.

Among the list of hot-shit components is the aluminum swingarm from Brock's Performance, supported by piggyback Ohlins shocks. Seventeen Lyndall wheel is wrapped with a 170/60-17 tire from Avon.

Chapter Twenty One

Aged Like a Fine Wine

Some bike-building projects simply take longer than others to achieve the desired result. For Greg Wick, the building of his FXRT took years instead of months. The idea for the bike you see on these pages started in early 2015 when he and long-time friend Brian Klock were discussing an appropriate ride for the upcoming Hot Bike Tour. They had collaborated on a number of notable builds in the past and one of their favorites was the FXRV, a V-rod turned FXR type tourer. "We decided to put a modern spin on a tried and true FXRT and wanted a nice stock bike to start the project," explains Greg, "I found this absolutely cherry FXRC through a dealership in Wisconsin and Brian offered to pick it up for me. The bike was the personal ride of the service manager at Madison Harley-Davidson who uncrated it himself. Brian called me from the road with the bike in the back and his report was both good and bad."

Brian started with the good news, "Man, I'm looking at it in the rearview and this is the nicest FXR you've ever seen. The cables, the pegs, the paint, it's all PERFECT." Then came the bad news, "it's so nice, there is no way we can cut this one up, this is museum quality."

With mostly factory sheet metal and an Evo for power, Greg's RT might be called a classic FXR taken to the next level.

So, Greg sold the perfect FXR to Nick Trask – and to this day it sits in the Trask Performance showroom, because he can't cut it up either. Thus the search started all over again.

Bike number two was a 1991 FXRS, in nice – but not perfect – condition. "Remember we initially wanted to have the bike ready for that year's Hot Bike Tour," explains Greg, "but other commitments happened and we just couldn't get it done in time. Brian and I felt it was meant to be that the pressure was off - we could take as much time as we wanted to finish it. We worked on it off and on when it felt right."

"The goal," says Brian, "was to build what a car builder would call a tasteful "resto-mod." On the order of a classic 32 Ford or a 67 Chevy Pickup, we used some tricks for a throw back to the time when

No stock bars here, the Klip Splitters from Klock Werks are mounted to tall LS Choppers risers. Note the extension on the modified factory tank, and how it all blends with the Danny Gray seat.

This RT rolls on stock, cast wheels and Pirelli tires; a 100/90-19 up front and a 130/90-16 bringing up the back.

some of our heroes started customizing FXRs."

"The wheels for example, they're the factory wheels, cleaned up and painted to match the bike – Donnie Smith style. We thought through the touches to the sheet metal, swing arm and fairing to work together and complement each other to create balance".

The panel paint job is another throwback. Jeremy Seanor of Lucky Strike Designs began by spraying the beautiful PPG Black Cayenne for the main paint color. Jeremy then used his considerable talent to create the elaborate panels. The borders are silver leaf with an engine-turned pattern. Inside the borders is a fine wine-berry, and inside of that is more silver

Known for their work on Evos, Head Quarters overhauled the motor, including a rebuilt bottom end, bored out cylinders, HQ's own pistons, ported heads and HQ's 0029 cam.

To make sure it sat just right, the Klock krew lowered the RT one inch, and stretched it 2 inches by adding material to the swingarm.

103

The front brakes might have been borrowed from a Formula One car – six-piston calipers and 13 inch floating rotors is a hard combo to beat for stopping power, all from PM.

leaf. The pinstripes that run through the designs are teal, while red defines the silver leaf borders and is used to add some more of Jeremy's tasteful fineline pinstriping work in the fairing and on the saddlebags.

Keeping with the bike's theme, the V-Twin is an 80 inch Evo, with a "95" kit and cam from Doug Coffey of Headquarters fame. Feeding the hot-rod-80 is a massaged Keihin carb, while a Compufire ignition lights the fire, and a two-into-one exhaust from Super Trapp provides an efficient escape route for the spent gasses.

If there's one thing that's missing from those Evo powered FXRs, it's a sixth gear. The Klock Werks crew took care of that omission with the addition of a Baker six-speed tranny.

Though the bike came as an FXRS, Greg wanted the style and wind protection afforded by a signature FXRT fairing. Actually the fairing mounted to the frame on Greg's new ride started life bolted to a police bike, which meant the FXRP fairing came with the bulge where a radio once sat. Thus Brian and crew had to smooth out the top of the fairing – so it looks now like a genuine RT fairing. The lowers are original units, narrowed 2 inches.

The bands of silverleaf and graphics laid on the base paint of Black Cayenne really make each component pop.

Once Greg and Brian had the signature fairing taken care of, the clam-shell bags were added next, along with the small RT tour pac. When people started customizing the RTs, the first thing they did was delete the tour pac. Greg wanted to have both the extra storage capacity the tour pac affords - and the sleek looks of a RT without that big lump above the rear fender. The answer is a KW quick detach bracket, so anytime Greg wants to rock the minimal look all he has to do is slip off the tour pac.

The rest of the "sheet metal" includes a smoothed out FXR gas tank with a fabricated tank extension and a pair of one-off KW side covers. The front fender is from Russ Wernimont Designs. The rear fender is likewise a Russ Wernimont item, though it's been stretched to make room for the integral license plate mount, and embellished with a signature Klock Werks taillight.

All those parts, both plastic and steel, are fastened to a genuine Milwaukee-built FXR frame. There is no stretch to the frame or increase in the rake angle. The only thing that's stretched is the swingarm, which is now two inches longer than stock. Bolted to the neck is a 39mm Harley fork assembly lowered one inch with a Burly lowering kit. The other end is suspended by a pair of adjustable Legend REVO shocks.

Greg felt that the resto-modded project deserved some serious brakes. The Klock Werks team complied with two, PM six-piston calipers for the front wheel. The icing on the cake is the large-diameter floating rotors. As Brian explains, "PM doesn't make those big rotors anymore, but I called and somehow persuaded them to manufacture two, brand new thirteen inch rotors." For the rear wheel, Brian and crew installed a smaller, eleven inch floating rotor, matched with a four-piston PM caliper.

When it came to choosing a set of bars, Greg was faced with a quandary. His first choice would always be Apes, but not on an FXR. The trend of late for these bikes is club style bars. So, for another modded touch Brian fabricated a set of club-style bars using Klock Werks Klip Splitters. To accommodate Greg's reach, he made them TALL and mounted them in risers from LA Choppers.

Greg's new FXRT didn't make it to the Hot Bike Ride, but it did make it to a few rides during Sturgis 2019. When asked about the new bike, Greg has a very simple answer: "It's one of the smoothest I've ever ridden, the thing just works."

Builder	Klock Werks
Year/model	1991 FXRT
Engine, year, displ.	H-D 1991, 82 cu. In. Evo
Engine builder	Klock Werks
Cases	H-D
Cylinders	H-D
Heads	H-D, Head Quarters
Aircleaner	Drag Spec.
Exhaust	SuperTrapp
Transmission	H-D w Baker 6 Speed Gearset
Frame, stretch/rake	H-D, Swingarm 2 in.+
Fork Ass'm	H-D
Triple trees	H-D
Shocks	Legend Revo
Front wheel/tire	H-D, Pirelli 100/90-19
Rear wheel/tire	H-D, Pirelli 130/90-16
Calipers	Front PM 6 piston/13 in., Rear PM 4 piston
Sheet metal	Tank H-D, fenders RWD
Sheet metal mods	Klock Werks
Painter	Jeremy Seanor, Graphics Lucky Strike Des.
Paint brand	PPG

Yes, the stylized taillight molded into the fender is a Klock Werks item. And Jolene? It's an inside joke and has nothing to do with the Dolly Parton song of the same name.

Chapter Twenty Two

First Time Custom

To look at Bill Blackmore's custom, it's a little hard to believe that it all started with a stock 1991 FXRT. "I rode the RT for two years," says Bill, "I wanted to see if I liked the bike." Bill must have like the RT, because after two years, the bike became the foundation for a full-blown custom.

"I'd never built a custom," recalls Bill, "but I'd always dreamed about building a truly one-off bike. Not something assembled out of catalog parts." A background in the marine industry might not seem like a good foundation for bike building. When you consider however, that for 30 plus years Bill designed and fabricated parts from stainless and fiberglass, it's easy to see that he was no virgin when it came to design and the problem solving that goes hand-in-hand with any fabrication project.

Once he had the bike stripped down to a frame sitting on a hoist, Bill started the project by making paper patterns, "I was trying to see what I liked and what I didn't," says Bill. "I wanted to make my own bags, and once I had a basic silhouette I stacked particleboards of the correct size together until I had enough depth. Next, I working on the backside, grinding away the wood to create cavities for the

Not your normal FXR or FXRT, but underneath those unusual shapes lurks a FXR frame manufactured in 1991.

Taking years to finish a custom bike affords the builder time to try cutouts, and this fender or that – and really see how it looks, after one day or one month.

Some of the shapes that Bill tried ended up on the cutting room floor.

We've all seen polished, beautiful V-Twins from S&S, but how many of us have seen…

The scratch-built bags were one of the hardest parts of the build and required a three-piece mold for each bag.

The fairing, now known as The Wedge, was a byproduct of the build.

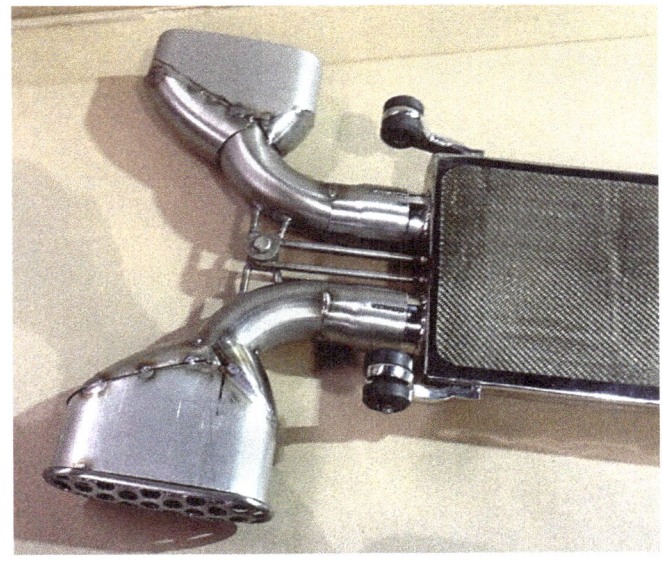

…A one-off exhaust system routed under the chassis.

A nice profile, aided in part by the bike's length – the frame is stretched 2 inches and the rake was modified 35 degrees.

A spin off from the build, the Wedge is a frame-mounted design meant to provide protection for riders of medium sized bikes.

shocks and anything else was going to get in the way of the bags. Once I had the clearances and basic shape right I took a belt sander and started shaping the outside of the bag, the part everyone sees. About half way through, I split the stack of particleboards, and inserted a metal sheet in the middle. That was done so that I could pop it apart later and make a two-piece mold. In the end we made three molds for each bag; two for the bag and one for the door. I fabricated the hinges from stainless."

The back fender is a Russ Wernimont product, but of course it didn't just bolt right on. "We welded in a separate inset for the license and taillight. Before calling it done I had to stretch the fender twice to make it accommodate the bags, and to make room for the hidden oil filter and rectifier.

What might be called a touring front fender is a Brian Klock product. Because it was designed for a Bagger, Bill had to split it down the middle, and remove a strip of material to make it a good bit narrower.

"The gas tank," explains Bill, "is from Fat Katz in California. I just shipped Don Baumunk the frame – already stretched two inches with six degrees of additional rake by Donnie Smith - and he sent it back with the tank in place. It was after the tank came back that I decided on another major frame modification, to drop the seat area four inches. The position of the tank and the dropped seat left a hole just behind the tank, and that's where we put the ignition panel. Normally the oil tank would be in that area right under the ignition panel, but we relocated the oil tank which meant there was plenty of room to hide the wiring in that area."

For power, Bill didn't want the stock Evo. And a leaned-on 80-inch Evo wouldn't be enough either. About the time he was considering his options for power Bill heard about a fully polished 110-inch S&S motor with less than 200 miles on the clock.

Bill bought the problem S&S motor at a huge discount and took it home. Once there, he pulled off the top end, and the fix was easy. Bill installed new head gaskets and rocker box gaskets. The only thing wrong with the engine was the original owner – who didn't believe in breaking in a new motor. In fact, he really liked to do smoking burn outs on his new bike with the new engine.

For the other major part of the drivetrain, Bill chose a complete Evo Bagger five-speed transmission with a polished case. The big advantage of the Bagger tranny was the location of the oil tank - underneath the tranny - much like the more modern Twin Cam bikes.

With the motor set in the frame and most of the sheet metal in place, Bill was faced with the challenge of an exhaust system. Knowledgeable riders that see the bike for the first time assume the pipes are on the other side. Until they walk around

The base paint of silver and blue, and the tasteful pinstripes, are the work of the Lenni from Krazy Kolors.

Arched gas tank is a one-off fabrication; note the ignition panel visually connecting the tank to the seat.

to that other side and realize that the pipes aren't there either.

"Being a contrarian," explains Bill, "I wanted to put the muffler and most of the exhaust under the bike. People said I couldn't do it. So I did it. People don't do it because it's expensive and time consuming, and mine was both. I like the idea of placing the exhaust under the bike. That way you can lean without ever dragging the exhaust because the clearance never changes."

"We built the muffler from scratch. In fact we made two or three mufflers before we got it right. The two pipes – also built from scratch - dump the exhaust into a common plenum, then it's routed through a set of baffles and out to

Handlebars are from Ness, as are the switches and hand controls.

Valanced front fender is a Klock Werks design —designed for Baggers it had to be narrowed to fit. Tubes are from Works, 4 inches over.

the turnouts on either side. Of course it's all stainless steel. And like some of the other sheet metal parts of the build, the muffler would have been much harder to fabricate without the help of a very good welder and fabricator by the name of Al Noard."

At this point the bike was essentially all there, but there was still one large part, and even larger project, to be finished.

Though he's owned a wealth of bikes both stock and custom, everything from a stock Ducati to a hardtail custom with a 145 for power, Bill likes a bike with a frame-mounted fairing. His first attempt was to buy a Road Glide fairing, but it was way too big. The obvious answer was to build one from scratch.

So, as Bill tells the story, "I cut up the Road Glide fairing to reduce the size and glassed it back together. Then I used that plug to make a fiberglass mold and I made the first fairing. But it wasn't right so I made another mold and another fairing. And then I did it all again and again until I finally got a fairing with a shape that looked good on the bike."

With a complete frame, driveline and body parts, it was time to finish up the chassis. Like a lot of us, Bill likes to surf the net looking for almost anything with something to do with motorcycles. "I found a rear wheel that was unlike anything I'd seen and wide enough to run a 150X16."

"The problem was trying to find a matching wheel," explains Bill, "which proved to be impossible. So I took the rear wheel to John Trutnau and asked him to make me a front wheel that would match the other wheel. John did a nice job, and turned out an eighteen-inch wheel, perfect for a 100X18 Avon. While he was at it, I had him make matching rotors for both

Speedo and tach are from the Drag Specialties catalog.

wheels. For calipers, I used chrome-plated Harley calipers."

The fork assembly came from Works, a combination of tubes four-inches over, with chrome plated lower legs. The rear shocks from Progressive are twelve inches long. The handlebars and grips carry the Arlen Ness logo, the simple two-gauge mount is from Drag Specialties.

The blue and silver paint job is the work of Lenni Schwartz. After all the bodywork was finished; Lenni sprayed all the chassis components with PPG silver. After some careful masking he spayed the GM blue over the silver, to create a paint job that fits the bike like a glove.

"It took me six years to finish the bike." Says Bill. "When I still had the marine business I kept it on a hoist in the back of the shop, and we'd work on it when things were slow. Really though, I couldn't get it finished until I retired and had more time. The bike was an on and off project. I wanted a nice distinctive motorcycle and I had no timeline - it took as long as it took to meet that goal. So the reality is, it's probably not done yet."

Builder	Bill Blackmore
Year/model	1991 FXRT
Engine, year, displ.	S&S 2017 110 cu. In.
Engine builder	S&S
Cases	S&S
Cylinders	S&S
Heads	S&S
Aircleaner	S&S
Exhaust	Custom, all fabbed from stainless
Transmission	H-D, Evo Bagger 5 speed
Frame, stretch/rake	1991 H-D, 2 in. 35 deg.
Fork Ass'm	Works, 4 in. over
Triple trees	H-D
Shocks	Progressive, 12 in.
Front wheel/tire	John Trutnau, Avon 100/100-18
Rear wheel/tire	Custom, Avon 150X16
Calipers	H-D
Sheet metal	Custom
Sheet metal mods	Bill Blackmore
Painter	Krazy Kolors, Lenni Schwartz
Paint brand	PPG

Under the bags are a pair of Progressive 12 inch shocks. Swingarm is stock; rear brakes use a H-D one-piston caliper and a custom rotor.

Chapter Twenty Three

An 'RT with Attitude

What's a motorcycle mechanic to do with a used FXR that he bought at a bargain price? If your name is Matt Anderson and you work at Gilby's Street Department in River Falls, Wisconsin, you might think it's a good idea to just fix it and sell it. "Flipping the bike was my initial idea," recalls Matt. "But then I started riding it, and doing burnouts, and riding it some more." He might still be riding it around on those Wisconsin two-lane highways except for one problem. "I did so many burnouts that I blew up the motor." After the big bang there wasn't much left of the Shovel's motor, so the FXR went into long-term storage in the back of Matt's garage.

"It sat there for a couple of years," explains Matt, "until finally I decided to do something with the bike. I started looking at other FXRs on the 'net, looking for ideas. There was this one that had a fairing and a lot of rake, I really liked the profile."

The key part of creating the new bike was the rake. "Once I had the bike stripped down and sitting on the lift, I cut off the neck and set it at 40 degrees," explains Matt, " After I welded the neck into the new position, I used a set of five-degree

Matt's RT is another of those labor-intensive builds, the result of an image on the 'net.

trees to reduce the trail, and a set of six-over tubes from Hard Chrome to make it sit level."

Once the frame was *fixed* Matt turned his attention to the motor. "I wanted to do something special, and at first I was going to use two small turbos, one for each cylinder. When I mocked it all up, however, it turned into a mess. Too many pipes. Then I got to messing with the heads, and ended up using two rear heads. That made it easy to route the exhaust right down the center and put the carb on the wrong side."

"Because the carb is on the left side, the intake ports had to be reshaped, which meant a lot of welding to fill in part of the port, and then grinding away material to finish the port. I cut the ends off an S&S intake manifold and welded those to the heads so the tubes coming from the carburetor had something to grab onto. But before I could weld the stub to the head I had to grind away some of the fins."

"There was also a problem with the angle of the pushrod tubes where they intersect with the bottom of the rocker box. I had to modify that area so the tubes had hole of the right size and at the right angle to connect with."

"I thought the camshaft would be a big problem, that I would have trouble finding someone to make a one-off camshaft, but Leineweber had dealt with this situation before and only charged me a hundred and fifty dollars extra to reverse the intake and cam positions for the front cylinder. The actual cam grind is designed for a big-inch Shovel. It's an E-5 with .580 inches of lift."

Because there wasn't much to salvage from the original engine, Matt used a 4-1/2 inch crank assembly and cases from S&S. The cylinders are Harley-Davidson 1200-Shovel cylinders. The actual bore size is 3.515 inches - after being bored .080 inches oversize. Filling those cylinders are two Wiseco 10.5 to 1 pistons, so the total displacement is about 88 cubic inches.

Hanging off the left side of the motor is the Weber DCOE 40mm carburetor. "It's a 40mm

Before paint, Matt set the neck at 40 degrees, and ordered a set of 5-degree wide glide triple trees to correct the trail.

Fork tubes are 6 inches over; lower legs are Softail-style from Arlen Ness. Chrome swingarm is stock length.

Gilby tapes out the graphic designs with the fairing on the bike - so everything lines up when it's all finsished.

carb," explains Matt. "I'm a Weber fan and I like the idea of a two throat carb, especially for this bike because there's one 20mm throat for each cylinder. Of course I fabricated the intake from 1-3/4 inch tubing – which just happens to be the same size as the exhaust pipes."

The exhaust that readers see on the bike is actually a condensed version of the pipes Matt built originally. As Matt explains the shorty pipes, "I fabbed up a nice set of drag pipes. They came down between the cylinders and then stretched back to about the beginning of the rear wheel. I sent them out to be chromed, but when they came back they were so thin from the polishing that they cracked right away. So I cut 'em short and wrapped them in exhaust tape."

The unusual Shovel uses two rear cylinders, which means the area where intake manifold would be is occupied by an exhaust pipe.

The 40mm Weber carb hangs on the left side and feeds what is now the front cylinder from the front side. BDL belt and clutch assembly live under the primary cover.

Wheels are from RC, a 21 up front and 18 in back. A single HHI caliper squeezing a RC front rotor, and a combo sprotor on the rear makes for a nice clean view from this side.

The transmission is a mostly stock 1982 five-speed, under the primary cover is a BDL belt drive and clutch assembly. A hydraulic master cylinder controls the clutch; part of the Accutronix forward controls, and shifting is done by the piston/shift lever seen on the left side.

The sheet metal on Matt's unique RT comes from a variety of sources. The tank is a stretched Drag Specialties item, while the front fender is from Klock Werks and the long rear fender is a Rick Doss item that Matt had to section the long way as it started out too wide for Matt's 130 rear tire. Stretched

The sprotor and matching caliper are from the V-Twin catalog. Wrap-around fender is a Rick Doss design; taillight and license bracket is Arlen's. The vented side covers are from Outlaw Cycles,

between the tank and the rear fender is a Perewitz signature seat from Mustang.

The bike came without a fairing, so Matt purchased an aftermarket fairing from Conley. "The upper mounting bracket came with the fairing," says Matt, "but I had to fabricate the lower bracket. In the end I changed the position and angle of the fairing until it sat right and lined up with the tank. Because the fairing was meant for a narrow-glide fork and I was using a wide glide I had to modify the fairing to make clearance for the tubes and trees. The other problem with the fairing was the lack of a real inner fairing, so I also had to fabricate panels for the speakers and the stereo head unit."

The rest of the chassis is made up of a stock swingarm supported by 12 Inch shocks from Progressive. Up front is the six-inch-over fork assembly already mentioned, with Softail lower legs from Arlen Ness. The single front brake assembly is made up of a HHI four-piston

Looks like a bad-ass motorcycle coming your way – chin fairing from Conley (manufacturer of the fairing), helps to fill the space between the front tire and the down-tubes.

Avon tire is stamped 90/90-19, covering the tire is a Wrapper fender from Klock Werks.

Builder	Matt Anderson
Year/model	1982 FXRS
Engine, year, displ.	H-D, 88 cu. In. Shovel
Engine builder	Matt Anderson
Cases	S&S
Cylinders	H-D
Heads	H-D
Aircleaner	Redline
Exhaust	Matt Anderson
Transmission	H-D 1982, 5 Speed
Frame, stretch/rake	1982, 0 stretch, 40+5 deg. Trees
Fork Ass'm	Pro One, 6 in. over, Ness lower legs
Triple trees	Pro One, Wide Glide
Shocks	Progressive, 12 in.
Front wheel/tire	RC 21X3.5, Avon 90/90-21
Rear wheel/tire	RC 18X4.5, Avon 130/80-18
Calipers	HHI
Sheet metal	Tank, Drag, Front KlockWks, Rear Doss
Sheet metal mods	Matt Anderson
Painter	Gilby
Paint brand	H of K

caliper mated to a RC rotor designed to match the 21-inch Nitro wheel. The rear brake is a "sprotor" item, both the caliper and the rotor/sprocket came out of the V-Twin catalog. Like the front, the rear wheel is from RC, only this one is eighteen inches in diameter.

You don't see many sprotors of late, except on choppers, but Matt had a good reason for using one on this FXR. "I really like those wheels, and by using a single front rotor and caliper mounted on the left side, and incorporating the rear brake into the rear sprocket, the view from the right side really shows off those wheels without anything in the way."

Once Matt was sure everything fit, he turned all the pieces over the Gilby for the paint. A big believer in House of Kolor, all the materials from the primer to the clear are from that same legendary paint company.

After applying and sanding the H of K primer, Gilby spayed on one coat of sealer, and then the real fun began. "We use two different base colors," explains Gilby, "Cinder Red BC 11 on the frame and some of the sheet metal, and Planet Green BC 09 on the rest of the body parts. Then we used one color of kandy topcoat, Tangerine Kandy UK 08, on all the parts. I applied 4 to 6 coats of the kandy followed by 3 coats of clear. After sanding I did the gold leaf, followed by more clear, then pinstripes and the graphics in black. The last coats I applied were another six coats of clear before I could do the final buffing."

The finished project is a long ways from the early FXR that Matt had as a starting point. The new bike handles just fine, with no flop from the extra rake. Power-wise, what was a well-worn Shovel is now a hot Shovel of nearly 90 cubes with extra compression and a high lift cam. Which brings us around to one thing about this bike that is like its predecessor — it's a great bike for doing burnouts!

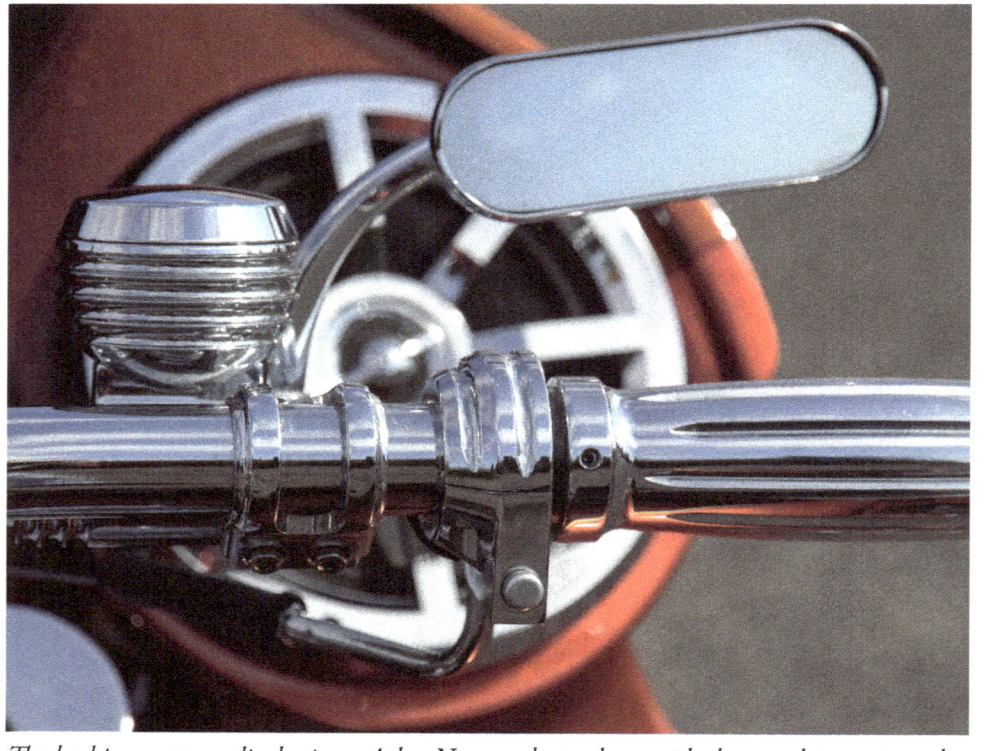

The beehive master cylinder is an Arlen Ness product, along with the matching grip and mirror.

Chapter Twenty Four

Dream Machine

Anyone who has built a bike, or tried to build the perfect motorcycle, understands the power of dreams. They also understand that reality often gets in the way of those dreams. Reality can manifest itself as money – as in not enough. Or it can show its ugly face as time – again a case of not enough.

Wes Adams falls into the second group. Shortly after purchasing a Paucho FXR frame from Dave Perewitz, along with wheels and sheet metal, he changed jobs. The new job promised more money, but less time at home.

Wes soon learned that when your construction job takes you out of town for weeks at a time, it's tough to get anything done in the garage at home. Thus he was faced with the dilemma. Sell the parts, let 'em rust in the garage, or find someone to finish the bike.

Deciding to hire someone else to build the bike was the hard decision. Deciding who should be the one to do the work was relatively easy. "I've known Gilby (of Gilby's Street Department) for a number of years," explains Wes, "and I always liked the bikes that came out of his shop."

"When he dropped off the project at our shop there really wasn't much to see," recalls Gilby. "Wes had an aftermarket FXR frame with 35 degrees of rake and two inches of stretch. Also a fork assembly, fenders, a gas tank, two wheels from DNA and a few miscellaneous items.

"The first thing we did was assemble the rolling chassis. If all the chassis components would work

Longer than most, Wes' FXR is based on an aftermarket frame with a 2 inch stretch, a 35-degree neck and a set of 5-degree trees.

The first thing Gilby did was strip the mocked up bike to a bare frame and make sure the frame was OK.

Triangle under the seat is another fabrication from aluminum; note the rolled edge to give it a softer border.

The extended side covers were made from light board, and then the dimensions were transferred to sheet aluminum, attached with brackets.

Gilby fabbed the housing and eyebrow for the Cycle Vision light and license bracket, and welded it to the fender.

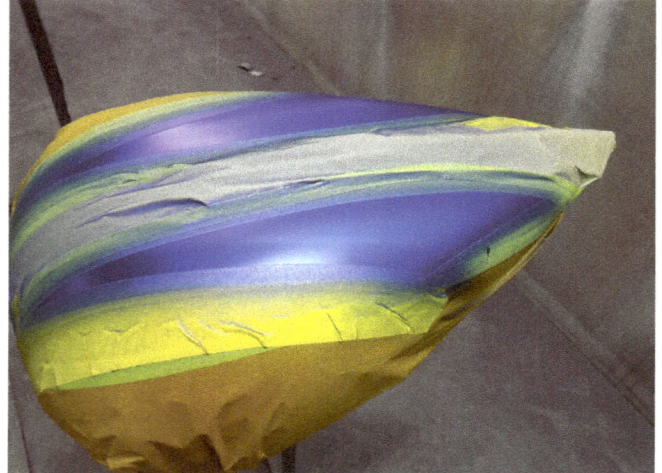

Anyone who's watched the taping and retaping that's involved in a custom paint job comes away with a new appreciation of the steps that goes into a custom paint job.

The sculpture on the back fender butts up against the seat and essentially continues the shape almost to the taillight.

The missing FXR oil bag means no bulge under the seat, and a very clean and sanitary Evo just standing there alone for all the world to see.

together then we could do the full mock up. The big problem I saw right away was the front end. Wes had a mid-glide assembly including triple trees without any rake. I called Wes and explained that we needed more rake in the trees to get the correct trail. And that there were no raked trees available for a mid-glide fork. We ended up using a complete wide-glide fork assembly from HHI, with a set of five-degree triple trees."

The rest of the chassis components were all there. The front wheel measured 21X2.75 inches wrapped

Note how the seat is captured on either end, and becomes a very integral part of the motorcycle.

with a 120/70/21 from Cobra. Wes wanted a pro street look, so the rear wheel measured 18X5.5 inches, wide enough for a 200/55/VR18 tire, also from Cobra. One of the advantages of buying an aftermarket frame is the fact that they come with options. Like a wide rear frame section and matching swingarm, which makes it easy to install a fat rear tire without modifications. For brakes, Wes picked GMA calipers, one on each end of the bike. The wheels, rotors and rear sprocket all came from DNA.

As Gilby explains the process, "Once we changed out the fork and assembled the rolling chassis we went ahead and fit the sheet metal items. I added sculptures to the top of the tank and also the top of the rear fender. I also fabbed an eyebrow in the rear fender over the taillight from Cycle Vision. When Wes stopped by the shop to check out

The 21-inch wheel is from DNA wrapped in a Cobra 120/70-21 tire. Single disc brake is a combo of GMA caliper and DNA rotor.

Seen in the paint booth – here's the tank with Gilby's finished designs in both two and three dimensions.

the bike he liked the work we'd done. After that visit he gave us free reign, told us to just keep going. It was at that same meeting that Wes found a certain blue in the House of Kolor sample book – and that Stratton blue became the dominant color for the whole bike."

When it came time to finish up the sheet metal, Gilby decided not to buy any of the side panels available from the aftermarket, he decided instead to make his own. "We made the covers from aluminum," recalls Gilby. "I made the triangle-shaped side cover to fit inside the frame tubes under the seat. Then I thought, 'no one does anything with the area under the triangle.' So I mocked up some light board and when I liked the shape I transferred the shape to aluminum. Essentially it's an inverted triangle with a trailing edge that follows the radius of the wheel."

The only piece of sheet metal that wasn't modified on Wes' new bike was the front fender from RWD, the one that wraps snuggly around the twenty-one inch tire.

For an engine Wes found a 80 inch Evo from a 1989 FXR. For a transmission, he wanted a five-speed from a Evo powered Bagger, and found one in a parts yard. Once delivered to Gilby's, main-mechanic Matt disassembled the Evo so key components, like the cylinders and heads, could be cleaned up and coated with charcoal-grey powder. Like the Evo, the case for

The majority of the hardware seen here is from the Arlen Ness catalog: headlight, handlebars, and mirrors. Master cylinders carry the PM logo.

No typical chrome fender strut with this Paughco frame. Brake assembly is another GMA-DNA combination. Gilby took license with the FXR design, adding the lower sheet metal.

Builder	Gilby Street Department
Year/model	2017 FXR custom prostreet
Engine, year, displ.	1989, 80 cu. In. Evo
Engine builder	H-D
Cases	H-D
Cylinders	H-D
Heads	H-D
Aircleaner	S&S
Exhaust	
Transmission	H-D 5 Speed, 1998 Road King
Frame, stretch/rake	Paughco, 2 in, 35 deg. + 5 deg,
Fork Ass'm	HHI Wide Glide,
Triple trees	HHI w 5 deg.
Shocks	13-1/2 in.
Front wheel/tire	DNA, Cobra 120/70-21
Rear wheel/tire	DNA, Cobra 200/55-18
Calipers	GMA
Sheet metal	Tank, Demon Cycle. Fenders, RWD
Sheet metal mods	Gilby
Painter	Gilby
Paint brand	H of C

the five-speed was treated to grey powder coat and chrome covers.

Though it does have turn signals and a horn, the wiring on Wes' machine is still pretty simple. The harness is the creation of Matt, and of course all the wires are hidden either in the tubes or handlebars.

Gilby's is a one-stop shop and when it came to paint, all the work from start to finish was done in-house. The Shimrin 2 is a House of Kolor product. Gilby sprayed the Stratton Blue over a grey base. Then the fun really began. The fenders and the tank all have a multi-layer graphic. And the sheet metal components have a quarter-inch wide silverleaf graphic tinted with Oriental Blue Kandy that follows the metal's shape. And of course once all the taping and spraying were done Gilby applied multiple coats of clear followed by a careful buffing session.

If you ask Wes, there isn't anything he'd change. The bike looks good, runs well and handles well partly because of the careful attention paid to the rake and trail numbers.

Wes' Evo is an 80-inch model, originally in a 1989 FXR. Matt disassembled the top end so the cylinders and heads could be powder coated, but otherwise left the motor in stock condition.

Wes did hit one snag that came about at the end of the building process. Even though all the parts were bought from legitimate sources, the paper work for the engine (which came out of another Harley) did not pass muster with the DMV. It was definitely a hassle to straighten out, and the last thing anyone wants to do when faced with a brand new bike that can't be ridden legally. All mentioned here only as a message to all the readers – be careful with the paper work when building an aftermarket bike.

Chapter Twenty Five

FXR CVO Specials

According to experts, the old story that Harley launched CVO to use up a pile of FXR frames they found in a corner - is not true. The tooling was on hand, and the bikes could be built for a limited run without disrupting regular production. Since then the reputation of the FXR as "best Harley ever" has stuck, and in the minds of former and current owners; it's probably the truth.

The FXR was brought back in 1999 when Harley Davidson launched its CVO (Custom Vehicle Operations) program with two models; the FXR2, with a 21-inch laced front wheel and 16 inch chrome cast rear wheel - and the FXR3, with chrome, spoked cast wheels on both ends, a 19-inch front wheel, and 16- inch rear wheel. Both machines were delivered with front and rear disc brakes, and both use one, single-piston, early-style caliper on the front, and the same caliper on the rear. Harley produced 900 FXR2, and 900 FXR3 models.

CVO was intended to produce exclusive low-volume custom bikes. For the model year 2000 approximately 900 FXR4s were produced; 300 in Candy Tangerine, and 600 in Screaming Yellow Pearl marking the end of the FXR production. The

A pristine FXR4 painted Candy Tangerine. Paint color and wheels are the primary differences between the FXR2, 3 and 4.

Mike's FXR4 came with almost zero miles on the odometer, and a spoked 19-inch front wheel and solid, cast 16-inch rear wheel. Note that Mike's FXR4 came with H-D's 4-piston calipers.

CVO FXRs used trick mirrors and grips, as well as chrome switch housings.

FXR4 differs from its close kin with the spoked, 19-inch spoked front wheel, and cast (solid) 16-inch rear wheel - though there seem to be a few 4s with the cast front wheel. Harley equipped the FXR4 with two of the then-new, four-piston calipers on the front, and one of the same on the rear. It was the last year Harley-Davidson would put an Evolution motor into a frame. All three FXR specials use mid-controls and highway pegs, and all three came with 39mm fork tubes. The Candy Tangerine example you are looking at was found with only 7 miles on the clock and in "brand new" condition; a once in a lifetime find!

Mike Johnson

No longer a perfect stocker, Chris' FXR4 uses the same wheel combo seen on Mike's bike, along with controls, sheet metal and gauges.

Chapter Twenty Six

A Replacement for the FXR

Design work on the Dyna as a replacement for the FXR started after the first FRX bikes hit the market. The word Dyna means power and is derived from the Greek word "dynamis". The first Dyna was introduced in 1991 with the limited production FXDB Sturgis model. The engine mounting system was changed from three rubber mounts to two, resulting in faster production on the assembly line; but unfortunately resulted in poorer vibration control. (It should be noted that before the Dyna, the company introduced the Wide Glide – FXWG - in 1980. The bike had the custom look and feel that made Harley Davidson motorcycles so popular. The Wide Glide sported a fuel tank with a flame paint job, a spoked 21 inch front wheel, and a wide front fork. The FXWGs had a bobbed rear fender, ape hanger handlebars, stepped two-up seat, and mini and forward mounted controls, giving it a distinct chopper feel. One could arguably assert that the FXWG was also a predecessor to the Dyna line.)

The limited edition Dyna FXDB Daytona and the FXDC Dyna Glide Custom were introduced in 1992. Apart from the paint scheme, the Dyna Glide Custom was virtually identical to the Daytona.

Like FXRs, Dynas are easily personalized. Changes to Neil's 2007 Dyna include a black paint job with flames and black powder on most of the chassis parts including the spoked rims.

Dyna Customs were painted black and silver, and the early models had a silver powder coated frame. Later production frames were black.

The FXRT Sport Glide was discontinued in 1993 and the FXRS Low Rider was replaced by the FXDL Dyna Low Rider. The FXR, FXLR, FXRS-Convertible and the FXRS-SP Low Rider Sport continued to be sold and the FXDWG Dyna Wide Glide was introduced. The Low Rider Sport was discontinued in 1994, and the Low Rider was discontinued after the 2009 model year.

In 1995 the FXD Dyna Super Glide and the FXDS Dyna Glide Convertible were introduced. These Dynas replaced the FXR Super Glide and the FXLR Low Rider Custom, which were the last FXR models in regular production.

1999 saw the introduction of the new Twin Cam motor across the Dyna Family. The FXDX Super Glide Sport was introduced with improved suspension components and triple disc brakes. The FXDX-T Super Glide T-Sport, with a fork mounted fairing and improved detachable saddlebags, replaced the FXDS Dyna Glide Convertible in 2001, and was discontinued in 2003. The FXDC returned to the line in 2005 as the Super Glide Custom.

A new Dyna chassis was introduced in 2006 along with a new six-speed transmission. Other new models were the FXDBI Street Bob (a minimal, single seat Dyna Glide motorcycle available in the new 'denim' (matte) black color) and the limited edition FXDI35 35th Anniversary Super Glide (colored to resemble the original white 1971 Super Glide). The FXDX Super Glide Sport was discontinued that year.

In 2007, the Twin Cam 88 engine was replaced by the fuel-injected 1584 cc Twin Cam 96 engine across the entire Harley-Davidson Big Twin lineup, including the FXD series. The 'I' model designator was dropped for all models, since all Big Twins from then on had fuel injection.

The FXDF Fat Bob was introduced in 2008. In the same year, the FXDWG Wide Glide was sold as a limited edition 105th Anniversary model before being retired, re-emerging in 2010 with a different (bobber) rear treatment. 2010 also saw the discontinuation of the FXD base model (replaced by the FXDB) and the loss of the FXDL Low Rider. 2012 saw some Dynas obtain the TC103 engine, available in the FXDF and FXDWG models as well as the new FLD Switchback.

Harley-Davidson discontinued the Dyna platform in 2017 for the 2018 model year. They were replaced by a redesigned Softail chassis; some of the existing models previously released by the company under the Dyna nameplate have since been folded into the new Softail line. *Mike Johnson*

Another Neil project, this one started as a 2010 Low Rider, before being converted to a Switchback with correct front end, all sheet metal and black powder for the air cleaner and some chassis parts.

Chapter Twenty Seven

Sport Touring Dyna

When Shop Owner and long-time rider Kurt Peterson decide to build a new bike he set certain important criteria for the new machine. As Kurt explains: "I wanted some wind protection and comfort, but I also want to be able to give the guy in the other lane a run for his money. A road bike, but still fairly nimble."

The project got in gear when Kurt purchased a 2001, FXDX Dyna Sport. "I like those first years of the Twin Cams," explains Kurt, "because they came with Timken bearings in the left side of the engine cases. Those tapered bearings really give the crank a lot of support, in 2003 Harley went to roller bearings on both sides of the crank, and I just don't think those are as good."

Those early Twin Cams came out with only 88 cubic inches displacement. Kurt of course did the logical thing – punched the motor out to 95 cubic inches with bored cylinders and bigger pistons. At the same time he installed a performance cam

Kurt Petersen of Lil' Evil fame, was one of the first to hang FXRT components on a Dyna chassis. What started as a 2001 FXDX Dyna Sport evolved into a true Sport Touring bike.

The single biggest part of the conversion to Sport Touring is the frame-mounted fairing. Note the Dive Bars with factory switches mounted to a set of club-style risers.

and ported heads. All the engine work, including the porting, was done at Kurt's shop, Lil' Evil, in Perham, Minnesota.

The conversion from bare bones Sport Dyna, to something better suited to long days in the saddle started a few years after the purchase. "I already had a set of clam-shell bags," explains Kurt, "so I put those on, but of course they didn't just bolt right on."

The first problem popped up when Kurt realized that the shock location on his Dyna is was different than it is on a FXR chassis. In the end, Kurt made is own brackets for the bags, but that tuned out to be a whole lot of extra work: "Fabricating my brackets meant I could position the bags anywhere. I finally decided to mount them farther forward and lower than they are a FXRT."

Kurt left the frame stock, though the factory H-D tunable fork legs are mounted in 3-degree mid-glide trees from Accutronix. Shocks are Legend Revo A's.

The same situation popped up when Kurt decided to install a FXRP fairing on the Dyna. "This was before people were putting the FXR fairings on the Dyna chassis and a lot of people said it would look really bad. But I did it anyway. And just like the bags, I had to pretty much make the brackets and weld some bungs onto the frame. Again, the extra work of making brackets gave me the freedom to position the fairing lower, and closer to the tank than where it would have been had I just used some universal aftermarket brackets."

Because the fairing started life on a police ride, it came with a flat surface on the top of the fairing for the radio. Before painting the fairing, Kurt, with help from Doug Wozney of Dougz, eliminated the radio-mounting lump and also moved the gauges up into the fairing. Installing the crash bars took more cutting and welding; I wanted to use a Street Guide crash bar, but then the typical lowers wouldn't fit. In the end, we cut and rotated the bottom of the Street Guide crash bar so the HD bagger lowers would fit.

To most riders, all custom bikes have one thing in common – they're LOW! Kurt had other ideas. "My Dyna is a Sport, so it came with thirteen inch shocks in the rear, and fairly tall fork assemblies. But I like to go around corners and I also hate to reduce the amount of travel, for the sake of comfort. The bike still has thirteen inch shocks on

What started as an early 88 cubic inch Twin Cam is now a very healthy 95-inch V-Twin. Primary drive uses the stock Harley chain.

Under the S&S air cleaner lurks a Mikuni 45mm carb. Rated at 118 ft. lbs. the 95-inch motor uses 10.25 to 1 pistons, ported heads, and a Lil Evil special two-into one-exhaust system.

Builder	Kurt Peterson - Lil' Evil
Year/model	2001 FXDX Dyna Sport
Engine, year, displ.	H-D 2001, 95 cu. In. TC
Engine builder	Kurt Peterson
Cases	H-D
Cylinders	H-D
Heads	H-D
Aircleaner	S&S
Exhaust	One off, two-into-one
Transmission	H-D 5 Speed
Frame, stretch/rake	H-D stock
Fork Ass'm	H-D
Triple trees	Accutronix Mid Glide
Shocks	Legend 13 in.
Front wheel/tire	PM, Avon 100/90-19
Rear wheel/tire	PM, Avon
Calipers	H-D
Sheet metal	Stock, FXRP fairing w Bagger lowers
Sheet metal mods	Kurt Peterson
Painter	Dougz Custom
Paint brand	

back, and I slid the for tubes up in the triple trees, but just a little, enough to make the bike sit level."

Most people who look at the bike's profile will swear it is lowered, in spite of what Kurt says to the contrary. In reality the bike is lowered – visually. The lowered fairing and bags give the bike the long and low look – without the need to buy shocks or shorter tubes.

Like all worthwhile projects, this one took a long time. And like those projects this one was worth every dollar and all those late night hours. "When I bought the bike," explains Kurt, "it had 16,000 miles on the clock. This summer (2019) I expect to see the odometer roll over 200,000 miles. I own a number of bikes, but the one I usually grab, especially if it's going to be a long ride, is the Dyna.

It's almost 200 miles from my shop to the Minneapolis area if I want to ride with Donnie and the gang. Which means by the time I roll to there and back, and do the ride, it's a 600-mile day. And I do it with pleasure and come home ready to do it again the next day. That's the bike I had in mind when I started the project – one I could ride two or three long days back to back, without feeling beat up - and that's the bike I have today."

The factory clamshell bags are mounted with Kurt's own fabricated brackets. Taillight is a Radiantz L.E.D.; just above it is an H-D license bracket.

Chapter Twenty Eight

One Woman's Hot Rod

Everybody has their own idea of what a perfect motorcycle Hot Rod should look like. Lora Wilkinson, long-time rider and David Perewitz's significant other, carried a vague image of a hot rod motorcycle around in her head. And like the rest of us, it took her time - with help from David - to make the leap from that out-of-focus mental picture, to a real-life, two-wheeled motorcycle.

"We built a custom Softail, but it just wasn't the bike for me," recalls Lora. Next, David suggested either a Dyna or FXR," explains Lora. "And we finally found a Dyna Switchback with low miles at a good price. I liked the idea of having bags, and the size of the bike. It seemed like a good starting point for my new ride. There was only one real problem; I wanted better protection than you get from a windshield like the one that came with the bike. And when I looked, there just weren't many fairings available from the aftermarket."

The search for a fairing coincided with the introduction of a frame-mounted fairing called The Wedge. During Sturgis David and Lora talked to Bill Blackmore, the brain and energy behind The Wedge. Bill suggested Lora take his Dyna for a ride,

The addition of a Wedge, frame-mounted fairing, and a killer paint job by Dave Perewitz, helped Lora convert her stock Switchback into a cool, personalized mid-sized touring rig.

133

The Ness horn matches the air cleaner. Outer primary shines with black chrome. Mini-apes are likewise shiny black instead of chrome.

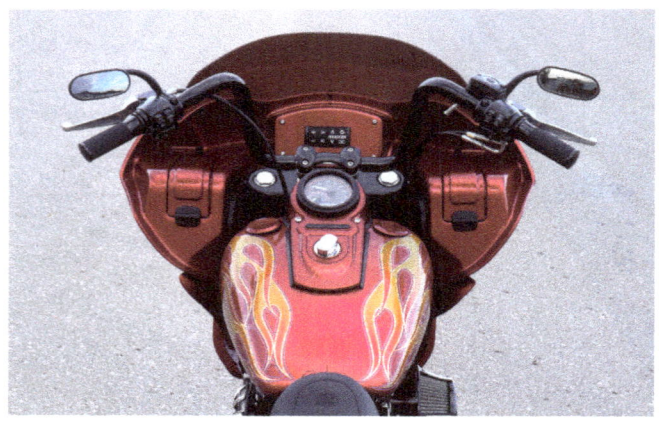

Compact Kicker stereo interfaces with a cell phone. Tank and dash are stock. Speedo with tach inset is from Dakota Digital, switches are from Milwaukee, mirrors are from Dublin, CA.

The Wedge fairing used two smaller headlights, and LED market/signal lights on either side. Red paint matches the original factory hue.

equipped with a Wedge, for a ride. And it wasn't long after that ride that Bill agreed to ship a Wedge to David and Lora as soon as he returned home.

Meant for mid-sized motorcycles, the fairing turned out to be the missing piece of Lora's Hot Rod puzzle. Her Dyna turned into a smaller version of a Road Glide. The fairing also created a larger canvas for paint. David started by painting the fairing Sunglow red to match the Dyna's factory paint. Next, he laid out a set of flames with overlapping licks that start at the front fender, before flowing across the fairing, tank and saddle bags.

For the flames, David started with a base coat of PPG silver metallic. Then he fired up his SATA airbrush to apply the actual gold-meets-red flames. With the whole PPG palette of paints at his disposal, David started with a yellow-gold candy at the front of the flames, and then came back and blended in the candy red for the licks.

A big part of building a personal hot rod involves the use of just the right, and just enough, accessories. It's as much about subtraction as it is about addition. In the subtraction category there's the rear blinkers, the stock air cleaner, the stock bars and the factory exhaust. In their place the crew installed a custom taillight assembly that eliminates the need for separate signal lights, an Arlen Ness air cleaner with matching horn cover on the other side, and a black Bassani two-into-one exhaust system. Black mini-apes replace the stock bars and give Lora what she calls, "better leverage and more comfort."

Lora knew that her hot rod required great tunes, but instead of a big AM/FM with CD head-unit, she requested a small, and simple Kicker system with two speakers and an additional amplifier. It integrates with her iPhone and offers a big bang from a small package. For gauges, Lora chose a Dakota Digital analog speedo with inset tachometer and all the standard warning lights.

One of the nice things about the Dyna chassis is the bike's relatively low seat height. For Lora, that seat height was lowered further with a shorter set of 440 shocks from Progressive. The stock wide glide front end was left stock and the combination means Lora is flat-footed while waiting for a stoplight. It also gives the bike a bit of that tail-dragger look popular with hot rods back in the day.

In the end it took two bikes to build one perfect machine. Along with one killer paint job, one new fairing, and just the right accents. Lora reports the bike is, "easy to ride, handles well, and looks great. I like the fairing, it keep the wind off, keeps me dry in the rain and makes it easy to hear the stereo."

Builder	Perewitz
Year/model	Dyna Switchback
Engine, year, displ.	103 cu. In. Stage I kit
Engine builder	H-D
Cases	H-D
Cylinders	H-D
Heads	H-D
Aircleaner	Ness
Exhaust	Bassani
Transmission	H-D 6 Speed
Frame, stretch/rake	H-D stock
Fork Ass'm	H-D stock
Triple trees	H-D stock
Shocks	Progressive, 11 inch
Front wheel/tire	H-D, Dunlop
Rear wheel/tire	H-D, Dunlop
Calipers	H-D
Sheet metal	Stock
Sheet metal mods	Wedge fairing
Painter	Perewitz
Paint brand	PPG

Metallic gold licks outlined with goldleaf (in place of 1-Shot) is hard to beat.

Chapter Twenty Nine

A Pro Builds One For Himself

Rick Ward didn't start out to build a Dyna. In fact, he started with a FXR. You have to understand that Rick's goals, as former crew chief and rider for the Vance and Hines team, are just a bit different than goals that the rest of us might set. "My intentions were to build the FXR with a 124," recalls Rick. "And then install a 143 at a later date. I wanted something I could race at the Chip during Sturgis. But then I learned that the S&S 143 won't really fit in a FXR frame – you have to do major surgery - so I bought a Dyna and built that instead."

Once all that was settled, Rick bought a clean 2009 Dyna Super Glide. Rather than buy a crate motor, Rick started with the Dyna cases and installed a crank assembly from S&S with a stroke of 4.625 inches. Though factory Twin Cams use a roller bearing on either side to support the crank, Rick chose to keep the roller bearing on the right and support the drive side with a pair of tapered Timken bearings. For cylinders, he chose two aluminum cylinders with a bore of 4.125 inches from S&S. To top off the cylinders, Rick CNC ported Harley Davidson MVA cylinder head castings.

When Rick Ward built this 124, he started with the cases original to the bike. The rest of the motor is partly Screamin' Eagle (heads, throttle body, air cleaner) and partly S&S (cylinders).

Ready to rock 'n roll, up front a 120/70-17 tire mounted on a Brock's Carbon rim, supported by a 'Busa inverted fork mounted in Brock's triple trees. Headlight is a Drag Specialties item.

If you wonder why he didn't buy two high-flowing heads from the aftermarket, it's because Rick runs Ward Performance and is known world wide for cylinder head design and porting. His customers range from racers building an American V Twin to the professional drag race teams including the team with the world's fastest Pro Street 'Busa.

To finish the Dyna's 124, Rick installed a Screamin' Eagle 64mm throttle body and S&S .675" lift cams to ensure the Twin Cam gets enough air, while the fabricated in-house two-into-one exhaust header makes an efficient exit route for the spent gasses.

In the rear, a 190/50-17 tire is supported by a +6 inch Brock's swingarm. Drag race shocks carry the JRI logo. Caliper is Brembo, fender is from the Dyna (modified) and a license housing from Drag.

To get the bike as low as possible, Rick removed the cast pieces on the lower part of the frame, and that gave them another inch. The castings protect the oil pan and are the mount for the mid-controls. So the crew had to start by reinforcing the lower rail with a second tube on either side. Next, they made a new oil pan that wouldn't hang so low, and a new set of pegs. "Building the rear-set pegs was one of the toughest jobs of the build," says Rick. "They had to be designed so the rider could get his feet into a tucked position, and do it without burning his feet on the muffler. In the end I made 3 or 4 versions of each piece before I got them exactly the way I wanted. Even though our specialty is cylinder heads and engine development, we have enough equipment in our shop to build almost any part of a motorcycle. We are able to carry out the fabrication process in our shop from start to finish. That way we don't have to try to communicate what we want to someone else, and hope they understood our vision."

Though the frame was left with stock dimensions and rake, Rick did make some serious changes to the chassis. The Dyna fork went in the spare parts pile, while a complete 'GSXR upside-down fork assembly took it's place.

The Suzuki fork assembly came with brakes, rotors and even a fender, and all those parts can be seen right here.

"I did have to use a set of Brock's triple trees to make the swap easy and get the correct amount of trail. We did use all of the fork assembly, including the brakes and even the fender."

At the bike's other end, Rick installed a swingarm from Brock's, stronger and lighter than the stock unit, and six inches longer as well. The shocks are from JRI, meant for drag racing. Considering the length of the wheelbase and the output of the engine, chain drive to the rear wheel seemed the only answer.

Both wheels are from Brock's again, made for incredible strength and lightweight from Carbon

The tank is one of the few original Dyna components – like the rest of the machine it's coated with numerous coats of black urethane and clear applied by Finishline.

Fiber. The rear wheel measures 17 inches tall by 6 inches wide, wide enough that a 190/50/ZR17 fits just fine. Up front the wheel measures 17 by 3.5 inches and carries a 120/70/ZR17 tire. Michelin Power One tires were used (the same tires 6 second 230 mph Pro Street Hayabusa's use).

The considerable power from the 124 V Twin passes through a stock Harley primary chain to a non-stock Bandit clutch and through a set of Harley gears.

Sometimes, builders of race bikes focus on the motor, drivetrain and chassis to the point where the aesthetics may suffer. Rick has a different approach: "At first glance the bike appears stock which is good but also bad. I strive to make any custom part of the bike perfect, like it would come from the factory that way…I'm also not into loud color and paint schemes and prefer a bike that looks like this - like it was always meant to be. If someone takes a long hard look at the bike and knows what they're looking at, my bike is far from stock."

There really are only three major components that came on the original Dyna – the cases, the gas tank and the frame. The front fender is from the Suzuki that donated its fork assembly. The rear fender is a modified Harley item, the struts fall into the same category. The paint job, and more important the prep work, is the work of Brian Gall of Finish Line Design using Xotic materials. The result can only be called flawless. After six months of hard work and too many late night sessions, Rick was the owner of one very fast yet streetable Dyna.

Is it fast? Well, the horsepower graph on the dyno sheet tops out at just a little over 160. So far, the best ET is 9.92 seconds @ 135 mph – and as Rick puts it: "That's with a 230-pound rider!"

Builder	Rick Ward, Ward Performance
Year/model	2009 FXD Super Glide
Engine, year, displ.	Ward Perf. 2009 124 cu. In. TC
Engine builder	Rick Ward
Cases	HD
Cylinders	S&S
Heads	H-D, CNC ported at Ward Performance
Aircleaner	SE Heavy Breather, Ward Performance
Exhaust	Custom, Ward Performance
Transmission	H-D 6 Speed 2009
Frame, stretch/rake	H-D, stock neck, Brock's +6 in. swingarm
Fork Ass'm	Suzuki GSXR inverted assembly
Triple trees	Brock's
Shocks	JRI drag shocks
Front wheel/tire	Brock's 17X3.5, Michelin 120/70-17
Rear wheel/tire	Brock's 17X6, Michelin 190/50-17
Calipers	Brembo
Sheet metal	H-D tank, front fender Suzuki, rear RWD
Sheet metal mods	Rick Ward
Painter	Brian Gall - Finishline
Paint brand	Xotic

Left side provides a good view of the Brock's loooong swingarm, and the chain drive. Under the very black primary cover lies an H-D chain connected to a Bandit clutch.

All photos by Don Kates, Shooters Images Inc.
don@shootersimages.com   don@dakates.com

Chapter Thirty

A Performance Dyna

Tom Keefer was faced with a pleasing dilemma: what to do with the S&S 124 sitting in the corner of his shop. Given that Tom had always wanted to build a Performance Dyna, the answer was simple – buy a well used Dyna and give it a heart transplant. "The 2001 Dyna I bought was beat up and just down right ugly," recalls Tom, "but the price was cheap and I really only needed the frame, title and transmission. I planned to sell everything else."

Tom had a great motor, but initially didn't know for sure what to use for a transmission. In the end he decided to keep the stock five-speed Harley-Davidson transmission. "I used to worry about it, but I've beat it hard for a couple of years now and the transmission still works just fine," says Tom. "What didn't hold up was the stock-style clutch, so I installed a lock-up clutch and it works great, no more hassles." Connecting the transmission to the rear wheel is a 530 chain, chosen for durability and the fact that a chain leaves room for a fat rear tire.

With the drivetrain choices sorted out, there were still so many additional choices to be made. For advice, Tom talked to Skeeter Todd, "and he got me thinking about lighter wheels," recalls Tom. "The issue was, I didn't have the budget for a pair of Carbon Fiber wheels. The answer was alloy wheels

What started as a beat-to-death mildly customized Dyna, came out as one fast, good handling Dyna with knock-out paint to boot.

The saddlebags were a swap meet special. They do fit so well - like they were meant for Tom's hot rod.

Even with a NAMZ harness kit, wiring can be a time consuming part of the project – one that should be done before the bike is finished. Tom did drill any necessary holes before paint.

The inverted fork, trick brakes and light alloy wheel were all parts of a metric ride at one time.

Handlebars and risers are both from Dynamic Dyna. Small reservoirs are meant for a ZX6R Ninja Kawasaki.

Later Dynas came with a longer tank. Installing one on an earlier Dyna is tough, but certainly makes for a nice profile.

Note the reinforced swingarm, the chain drive, and the stabilizer up front.

from a Metric bike, but I wanted to stay with a nineteen inch from wheel, and it's hard to find a Metric with a nineteen-inch front wheel. I finally discovered Suzuki's V-Strom which came with a nineteen in front and a seventeen in back."

The Suzuki wheels worked just fine, the rear was wide enough to take a 170/60-17 tire without complaint, and as Tom explains, "The Suzuki's rear sprocket ended up in a almost perfect location for chain alignment. All I had to do was use an offset sprocket on the transmission."

The rest of the choices Tom had to make ended up being a combination of modifying what he had, and cherry picking items from the used Metric market. To support the rear wheel Tom took option number one. It might not be as sexy as an aluminum swingarm but after reinforcing the Harley swingarm Tom saved some money and had the pride in knowing he did it himself.

To upgrade the front suspension Tom opted for option number two. "I bought a complete fork from a Ninja ZX 6R, luckily Brock's makes a set of triple trees designed to adapt a set of metric upside-down forks to a Harley. The install was easy and Brock's has figured out the trail, so there's no worry on that end. I bought the rear shocks from Brock's as well. They're tailored to the rider. All I had to do was give Brock the bike model, shock length and my weight."

Slowing down the kinetic energy of a 124 are three, four-piston calipers. Up front they squeeze two Galfer floating wave rotors, while the rear rotor is another Galfer wave design without the floating feature.

In terms of aesthetics, Tom found solutions that didn't fit option one or two. "I happen to know that the gas tank used on the later,

Tom just happened to have a complete 124 S&S Evo from S&S sitting on the floor when he started the project.

2005 Dynas is four inches longer than the earlier tanks. That extra length stretches out the profile, and comes from the factory with an aircraft-style gas cap."

The front fender is from a Deuce while the rear fender is one of the few original items other than frame and tranny that Tom didn't take to the swap meet. The saddlebags are older Harley items, discovered at the swap meet with a price tag of $50 including brackets. And the café-style quarter fairing is a H-D item, though Tom had to fabricate the brackets to make it fit an inverted fork.

The final step is the paint, and Tom had to ship the parts to Stoughton MA, home to well known painter, Keith Hanson. "I wanted what I call a dynamic paint job, with some old skool features - like pinstripes and goldleaf. And I don't think there's anyone who is better at that than Keith."

The first road test stretched from Pennsylvania to South Dakota, and was trouble free with the exception of a little clutch slippage. The good news includes the fact that the clutch did make the return trip – and Tom took home three awards from three different shows attended during the week. A pretty successful first road test.

Builder	Tom Keefer/Franklin Church Choppers
Year/model	2001 Dyna
Engine, year, displ.	S&S, 124 cu. In. TC
Engine builder	S&S
Cases	S&S
Cylinders	S&S
Heads	S&S
Aircleaner	Zippers
Exhaust	Vance & Hines Pro Pipe
Transmission	H-D, 2001, 5 Speed
Frame, stretch/rake	2001 Dyna stock
Fork Ass'm	Kawasaki ZX-6R inverted
Triple trees	Brock's
Shocks	Brock's
Front wheel/tire	Suzuki, Avon 110/90-19
Rear wheel/tire	Suzuki, Avon 160/70-17
Calipers	4 piston
Sheet metal	2005 Dyna tank, Duece front Dyna rear
Sheet metal mods	Tom Keefer
Painter	Keith Hanson
Paint brand	PPG

Not a show bike, this one's a runner – proven by the two trips from Pennsylvania to S.D.

Twin Cam/FXR Conversion Oil Pans
CNC machined from 6061 aluminum

- **INCREASED OIL CAPACITY**
  Over OEM oil bag

- **HARD ANODIZED & FINNED**
  For better heat dissipation & longer life - much needed with Twin Cam motors

- **LOWER CENTER OF GRAVITY**
  For better handling

Don't cut your FXR chassis for that Twin Cam/FXR conversion. Use the industry's trusted components - oil pans from Deviant Fabrications!

AVAILABLE IN THREE COLORS
Anodized Gold, Red & Black

www.Deviantfabrications.com
Instagram/Facebook
DeviantFabications

Nearly all titles published by Wolfgang Publications over the last 30 years can be purchased NOW.

Just punch the title into your browser. All books are printed in color (with a few exceptions) in the U.S. **Current titles are found at www.wolfpub.com**

MOTORCYCLES

H-D Twin Cam Hop-Up & Rebuild
H-D Evo Hop-Up & Rebuild
Advanced Custom Motorcycle Wiring
  - Revised
Custom Bike Building Basics: Tips for
  Backyard Mechanic
Custom Motorcycle Fabrication:
  Materials, Weld, Mill & Lathe
How to Build a Cheap Chopper
Build Your Own Bobber/Chopper
How to Fix Amer. V-Twin MC
Triumph MC Restoration: Unit 650cc
Triumph MC Restoraton: Pre-Unit
Vintage Dirt Bikes

PAINT PINSTRIPE AIRBRUSH

Advanced Custom MC Painting
Adv Custom Painting Tech
Advanced Pinstripe Art
How to Paint Tractors & Trucks
How-To Airbrush, Pinstripe &
  Goldleaf
Kosmoski's New Kustom
  Painting Secrets
Body Painting

AUTOMOTIVE

Hot Rod Wiring: How-To
How-To Chop Tops

TATTOO

Tattoo Bible Book 1
Tattoo Bible Book 2
Tattoo Bible Book 3

COMPOSITE

Composite Materials:
Fab. Handbook #1
Composite Materials:
Fab. Handbook #3

SHEET METAL FABRICATION

Advanced Sheet Metal Fab.
Learning the English Wheel
Power Hammers
Sheet Metal Bible
Sheet Metal Fab Basics

www.ingramcontent.com/pod-product-compliance
Lightning Source LLC
Chambersburg PA
CBHW041242240426
43668CB00025B/2461